PRAISE FOR THE MAN WHO IS
RESILIENT BY NATURE

"During all the years we played together, I was so impressed with Reggie's work ethic and dedication to being the best at whatever he did. He was all out. I'm also not surprised that he has fought challenges after football with everything he has. You hate to see him go through it, but if anyone can endure the type of obstacles and adversity he's faced, he's the one."

—ANTHONY MUÑOZ, Cincinnati Bengals
Hall of Fame tackle

"Reggie Williams epitomizes the Renaissance man. Intellectual. Athletically gifted. Passionate. Competitive. He raised the bar for everyone around him on the field and in the classroom. He made Dartmouth a better place, which is why we have a leadership award named in his honor. He is the best that we present and develop. It is no wonder that he's had impact in every endeavor he's taken over the course of his life."

—BUDDY TEEVENS, Dartmouth head football
coach and former teammate

"I have a huge amount of respect for Reggie. He never gives up. His ethics, honesty, and penchant for doing the right thing always impressed me. I never worried about him telling me what he thought. Kind of like my wife. I trust him."

—LEE COCKERELL, executive vice president
(retired), Walt Disney World Resort

"Reggie has been a trailblazer his whole life. Just an amazing leader. He would have been an out-of-the-box choice for the NFL, but with his business skills and savvy, I saw him as the ideal person to become the first African-American commissioner in professional sports."

—RICHARD LAPCHICK, founder of the Center for
the Study of Sport in Society

"Reggie was always more than just a 'football player,' evident by his serving on the Cincinnati City Council during his NFL career. He was true to who he was: the antithesis of every stereotype about a jock. Then again, how many NFL players are there from Dartmouth?"

—ANDREA KREMER, Emmy Award-winning
sports reporter

"He is one of the most astute and courageous sports personalities ever. His story is worth reading because it provides an architecture for success by persistence, hard work, and study. At different points in his life he faced discouragement, yet never let anything stand in his way. He has revealed to us all a certain genius."

—TYRONE YATES, Hamilton County (Ohio)
Municipal Court Judge

"There are not many people who will positively impact your life just by knowing them as Reggie does. One thing I love about him: he's not someone who climbed over people to advance. He brought people along with him."

—DAVID NEAL, executive vice president,
Fox Sports

RESILIENT BY NATURE

REGGIE WILLIAMS

WITH JARRETT BELL

Post Hill
PRESS

A POST HILL PRESS BOOK
ISBN: 978-1-64293-388-8
ISBN (eBook): 978-1-64293-389-5

Cover photo by Commander Kevin "Stainless" Steel, US Naval
Aviator 1984-2012

Interior design and layout by Sarah Heneghan,
sarah-heneghan.com

This is a work of nonfiction. All people, locations, events, and
situations are portrayed to the best of the author's memory.

Post Hill Press
New York • Nashville
posthillpress.com

Published in the United States of America

For my mother, Julia, and the memory of our wonderful soul mates, Eli and Kenny

CONTENTS

FOREWORD

WE GO THROUGH LIFETIMES, AND WE ALL LIVE DIFFERENT lives. Sometimes we live for a long time, sometimes we have a shorter time on this earth. My dad, Harrison Wilson III, died a little early, in my opinion. He was fifty-five when he passed away in June of 2010. But the reality is that my dad's legacy is forever. And it is forever within me.

Another part of my dad's legacy, part of who he was as a man, flows through Reggie Williams.

That's why I'm compelled to share a bit of the history between these two great men that resonates with me as Reggie reveals the depths of his own remarkable story.

Reggie and "Harry B.," as they called my dad, were football teammates at Dartmouth College—where my dad was a wide receiver and also played baseball. They were really close—the best of friends. Reggie was a big inspiration to my dad. But it went both ways. My dad gained a lot of knowledge from Reggie and vice versa. They shared a lot of wisdom and a lot of moments together. It remained that way through the years, long after their college days. That always stood out to me.

My dad never took character lightly. He loved people based on their character, not because of their status or accomplishments. That's why he had so much love for Reggie. I remember my dad talking about him all the time when I was younger and on into my teenage years. Obviously, Reggie was a talented football player and successful in business and other endeavors off the field, but what really sticks out from my dad's descriptions is that he is a person full of life, who cares deeply for others.

What a coincidence that I was born in Cincinnati—where my dad was a lawyer for Procter & Gamble and my mom, Tammy, finished nursing school at Xavier University. It also happens to be the place where Reggie became the greatest linebacker in Bengals history. He and my dad were able to reconnect and strengthen their bond in the years that their careers overlapped in Cincinnati.

Of course, I don't remember anything about their years together in Cincinnati; I was just over a year old when our family relocated to Richmond, Virginia. But my Uncle Ben has a bunch of stories off the top of his head. And as Uncle Ben once put it to a reporter, "Cincinnati is special, for connections long before Russell was born."

I'll take that.

It was also special that Reggie came to visit me a few months after my dad passed when I was playing in the Champs Sports Bowl in Orlando. It turned out that was my final game for North Carolina State before transferring to Wisconsin. We beat West Virginia, and what a game it was. I remember Reggie telling me, "Moving like your dad out there!"

I've heard that often from people who really knew my dad. Coming from Reggie, it meant a lot.

I can also relate to the physical challenges that Reggie has encountered in recent years—including the fight to save his leg from amputation—because of my dad. He went through those same challenges, the same tough moments. It's difficult for anyone, but particularly so when you're an athlete who's used your legs as part of your livelihood and what you've worked for your whole life. The moment that you learn you might lose your leg is a heavy moment. That was really tough on my dad, personally. Knowing that was a heavy weight on him in his life, I totally recognize how it has been a trial for Reggie too.

Reggie knows. The bond between my dad and him is forever. I'm grateful for that bond. I have a few people in my life with whom I have that kind of relationship. It helps that I've seen it firsthand. I'm grateful to Reggie and my dad for showing me what that kind of special friendship looks like between two talented, hard-working, high-character men.

I'm happy for Reggie in achieving another goal in telling his story, which surely captures his human spirit. Yet, much deeper than my sentiments, his old pal Harry B. would be so proud.

—*Russell Wilson*
Quarterback, Seattle Seahawks

INTRODUCTION

ROLL WITH REGGIE WILLIAMS TO CATCH A DRIFT OF THE
bustling activity at the restaurants and shops near Main
Street in tony downtown Sarasota, Florida, and it's like being
with the mayor.

The man has some presence. It seems that just about everyone knows him.

A restaurant manager embraces the imposing former
football player with a hug and, after a few minutes of chat-
ter, informs him that his drinks—including his favorite bour-
bon, Booker's—are on her. A bouncer outside breaks down
the details of a recent issue with patrons, keeping Reggie
informed of what sometimes happens when the place con-
verts to a club. A waitress, after stowing his crutches, wants
an update on the condition of his right leg, which pretty
much has a life of its own. Some people want to talk football.
Or baseball. Or basketball. Or even hockey. Any sport. Some
just shoot the breeze about their day-to-day issues. Or they
talk current domestic events. The gregarious man engages
with friends and strangers alike.

Williams, a divorced father of three adult sons, moved to
this cultural mecca adjacent to Sarasota Bay in 2017, primarily

because it felt right. He loves the water, the weather, the views from his bayside penthouse apartment, the vibe of the surrounding arts district, and the proximity to Orlando—close enough (a two-hour drive away) but not too close to his sons that he would be a burden.

It feels like home.

When he ambles into Bookstore One on the corner of Main and Palm, he is showered by a flood of love. It figures. This is one of Williams's favorite stops. That he is walking, albeit gingerly, is significant enough, given all that he's been through in recent years to save his ravaged right leg.

There were multiple threats of amputation, including one as recently as January 2019, four knee replacements, and twenty-seven surgeries. The toll of this has left the area of his right knee disfigured, scarred, and puffed up unevenly to the size of a melon, with no range of motion. Inside is a concrete spacer, while specially designed shoes equalize the right leg that is three inches shorter than the left.

The bookstore is also special because it was where, in early 2019, Williams was the featured attraction for one of the monthly community conversations it hosts. Williams built his session around the theme: what I'd put in my book.

The result has come to fruition to reveal layers of a rich, remarkable life—and that Williams can sure tell a story about his journey. He was once a star athlete revered for his relentless conditioning and Adonis physique. Now, he's an aging grandfather, challenging his battered body to keep up with a wise, youthful spirit that allows him to still compete—for the quality of his day-to-day subsistence, his legacy, his sanity.

"This is an inspirational way to recognize the life that I've lived," Williams reflects. "What I am going through has come with a lot of great memories. It's kind of like karma too. Because

I used to go to the library as a kid and always wondered, 'What section will my book be in?'"

Well, with his wide range of experiences, Williams's story isn't confined to one genre. Naturally, there's the backdrop of sports. He played fourteen years in the National Football League as a linebacker with the Cincinnati Bengals, including starting assignments in two Super Bowls. He is an Ivy League legend, the greatest player in Dartmouth's history, and an inductee into the College Football Hall of Fame. But it's also about politics. When he was a member of the Cincinnati City Council, he was the only active professional athlete to have served in such a significant governmental position.

It is about business too, given his role as an executive at Walt Disney World Resort in building the nation's preeminent youth sports facility—the ESPN Wide World of Sports Complex. This, after a stint as general manager of the anchor franchise of the World League of American Football. And after that, a stint with the NFL that resulted in the development of the first NFL Youth Education Town, in Compton, California—an outreach initiative attached to Super Bowl XXVII in the months following the Rodney King riots.

It is a tome that details too, one medical issue after another, most of which flow from injuries sustained in football, and Williams's means of coping—physically, mentally, emotionally, and spiritually—while battling assorted levels of red tape.

Essentially, though, Williams's story is that of a human being with tremendous gifts and, like all of us, flaws too, whose existence is woven together by a powerful thread of resilience.

"He is one strong man," Reggie's mother, Julia, said during the spring of 2019 as she sat in the den of the house in Flint, Michigan, where he grew up with his two brothers. "He comes from a lot of strong men. But he is in pain a lot. I'm coming from the mother's side. You hate to see your child suffering."

Julia believes the litany of health challenges has changed her middle son, although it also revealed much about his character as he remained determined to prevent amputation.

"He saved it for so long and worked with that knee," she said. "It's like it's his life right now. I know what he wants to do. I also know that some people think he should've given up on the knee and had the leg taken off. If they take it off now, they would have to go all the way up. That's frightening. He talked to his kids about it. They wanted him to go with the artificial leg. We all know that he could adjust if he did that."

Yet Williams, whose self-identity over many years has been built on the willpower of turning negatives into positives, will tell you that he wants a happy ending to his story. After enduring so many challenges to get to this point, he can't quit now.

"Reggie's always been fearless," declared his uncle Moses Williams, whose wife, Sadie, is the youngest sister of Reggie's late father, Eli. "He refuses to put the burden on anybody else. When we've talked about it, we use the Jim Valvano thing: Never give up. He says, 'I'm not giving up on this leg.'"

Reflecting on life certainly adds context to Williams's purpose.

Flashing back also uncovers at least one experience from his NFL career that remains stuck in his craw. Williams was the greatest linebacker in Bengals history, but he was never selected to a single Pro Bowl, let alone named to any All-Pro teams. He's also not crazy about failing to win a Super Bowl, but the Pro Bowl snub fuels a different type of disdain in his voice.

Let's go back to 1981. That was arguably Williams's best season—which ended with a trip to Super Bowl XVI in Pontiac,

Michigan, roughly thirty miles from his hometown—and was surely one in which he deserved a slot on the AFC (American Football Conference) Pro Bowl squad. He started all sixteen regular-season games and the playoff contests that season, and had career highs with eleven sacks and four interceptions while forcing four fumbles and logging three fumble recoveries.

The AFC's right outside linebacker for the Pro Bowl that season was Robert Brazile, who had lesser stats than Williams. And the squad included two left outside linebackers, Ted Hendricks and Bob Swenson. Meanwhile, the National Football Conference team included the rookie right outside linebacker who was all the rave that year, Lawrence Taylor (nine and a half sacks, one interception, one fumble recovery).

Williams doesn't discount Taylor's status as the greatest defensive player in NFL history—L. T. was the first linebacker to top Williams's eleven sacks from 1981—but it's fair for him to wonder why his production wasn't valued as highly in 1981, using a similar measuring stick.

"In that one year, the 1981 season, the demarcation between the best new thing that's happening in the NFL from linebackers and someone who's been here doing it for five years," Williams says, "was that one person in one market wasn't All-Pro and the other one, in the New York market, was not only Rookie of the Year but also All-Pro."

Still, Williams found a way to transform that negative into a positive. The snub inspired him to put more focus and energy into his community service efforts. There's no doubt that he became an essential All-Pro as a humanitarian, which resulted in the type of recognition that he never received for exploits on the field. He didn't pursue his community efforts, typically directed toward helping kids, to be honored. But that happened nonetheless.

Williams was, in 1985, the recipient of the Byron "Whizzer" White Award, the highest community service accolade of the NFL Players Association. He was the NFL's Walter Payton Man of the Year award in 1986, presented, ironically, at the Pro Bowl. In 1987, he was one of eight athletes named by *Sports Illustrated* as Sportsmen and Sportswomen of the Year, honored for their community service.

"When I came to the Bengals," said Joe Kelly, the former linebacker selected in the first round of the 1986 NFL Draft, "everything that I hoped I could be, he was already that."

Kelly now owns and operates five youth homes in the Cincinnati area that house children, many with abuse and/or mental health issues, who are wards of the state. Williams is on his board of directors.

Their bond extends to Kelly's rookie season, when he reported several weeks late to training camp after finally resolving a contract stalemate with the team. It was after Kelly's first practice when Williams, knowing the rookie didn't know a soul after a couple days in town, pulled up in the parking lot with his wife, Marianna, and his infant sons, Julien and Jarren, in the car with him.

"Hey, what are you doing the rest of the day?" Williams asked.

"Nothing," Kelly replied.

"Get in the car," Williams instructed.

The rookie was taken for a family outing at Kings Island amusement park.

"From that time on, he was like my mentor," Kelly said.

There is no shortage of testimonials from some of Williams's friends and/or teammates linked to various stages of his life, describing various traits:

— Ricky "Stick" Taylor, a childhood friend in Flint and teammate at Flint Southwestern: "He was an over-achiever. A great workout guy. And there was no quit in him."

— Rocky Whittaker, a former Dartmouth safety who was two years ahead of Williams: "Commanded mad respect. He showed up my senior year with his knee damn-near broke and refused to relinquish the opportunity to start at middle linebacker. And for a young guy not to waver in terms of taking a leadership role, he just did it. The void was there and we needed it."

— Ken Riley, the former Bengals cornerback: "His tolerance for pain was amazing."

— Anthony Muñoz, former Bengals tackle and Hall of Famer: "Unique. His commitment and work ethic was special. He'd come back from a city council meeting, and he was ready to go."

— Grayland Crisp, an Alpha Phi Alpha fraternity brother at Dartmouth: "When we were pledging, he took a stand for me when it looked like I was about to be kicked off line. When he stood forward, everyone else followed suit. He made it clear that we were all in it together. That's one reason why I'm indebted to him for life."

Williams realizes that inspiration goes both ways. Like with the phone call he received from former Bengals coach Marvin Lewis in 2013, on the day when the *Cincinnati Enquirer* published what turned out to be an award-winning account of Williams's challenges with his leg by Paul Daugherty. In the article, Williams—who was a pallbearer at the funeral of the legendary Paul Brown, founder of the franchise and father of team president Mike—expressed his frustration at the lack of support from the Bengals. He also mentioned that despite achievements ranking as the best for any linebacker in Bengals history, Williams didn't notice a single acknowledgment that he had ever played for the team during a visit to Paul Brown Stadium.

"Marvin was the first to call me that morning, and he said, 'We have not forgotten you,'" Williams recalled.

Then Lewis took it a step further, telling Williams, "If we win a Super Bowl, you're going to get my ring."

The gesture came at the right time, as Williams was in the throes of extensive rehab.

"That inspired me so much then," he said, "to dig deeper to overcome that stage of chronic pain, to rehab myself to where I could get off crutches."

Williams won't be forgotten. Instead, he'll always be remembered for his fortitude.

—Jarrett Bell
Lake Ridge, Virginia

CHAPTER 1

NIGHTMARE

I WAS ASLEEP, IN THE THROES OF THE MOST REALISTIC DREAM I've ever had.

I was in hell.

In my belief system, this nightmare was true to life. It happened. I was in hell for the mission of stealing my friend, Lenny Nichols, away from Satan. As I lay in a hospital bed in New York in April 2008 while trying to save my ravaged right leg, my essential existence was enveloped by every bit of the imagery of purgatory I have visualized and sensed otherwise: the smell; the sulfur; the pain; the agony; the flames; the depths of despair.

A single purpose drove me: I just had to get Lenny, this pure soul, out of a place that he did not belong. In my vision, I went in, grabbed Lenny, and proceeded to push him out. As I'm climbing out of hell, the last thing left was my right leg. That's when I awoke, and the leg was on fire. And you couldn't tell me that it wasn't literally on fire. Of all the trials this sixty-something-year-old body has endured—twenty-five knee operations, open-heart surgery, a stroke, agonizing biopsies to treat a bone infection, and an assortment of injuries during fourteen NFL seasons as a full-contact linebacker for the Cincinnati Bengals—it was the worst pain I've ever experienced.

As I hit the nurse's call button, the pain still wasn't as dramatic as the image of where I just was. I was in hell—with all the smells and the cascade of images. But the leg was still on fire. The doctor came in and took the Toradol—it's the strongest stuff they've got—and injected it right into my jugular. He said, "This is the best we can do for you. It should work for the pain."

It did nothing. Finally, a crew of about five or six—there were two doctors and maybe four nurses—came to witness my pain, agony, and writhing because it felt like my leg was literally on fire.

They were starting to discuss cutting off my leg when they gave me another Toradol shot in my jugular after twenty minutes—ten minutes earlier than the suggested timing between doses. It was that desperate. A shot to the jugular is the quickest way to get the medication into your bloodstream. But they did it twice, and neither worked. "Sorry, man, we're going to have to leave it for thirty minutes now."

I had to live with that excruciating pain and also with the fact that it was not a pain that mankind could eliminate. It was an evil pain. I was in the clutches of Satan. Earlier in my life, I'd helped exorcise demons from a couple of people. I'm an enemy of evil. This was me paying the cost: "How dare you!" For me, keeping my leg—threatened by amputation on multiple occasions—means keeping my sanity. And it's also part of my belief system that, by virtue of keeping my leg, I really did save the soul of my best friend, Lenny Nichols.

Oh, Lenny. Let me take you back further. Long before my resilience became such a major force in battling health issues and before significant careers in pro football and the corporate world, Lenny and I arrived at Dartmouth as members of the freshman class of 1972. We quickly formed a bond. Lenny was an All-State linebacker from Elmsford, New York. I was the kid from Flint, Michigan, with a chip on my shoulder after getting dissed by University of Michigan head coach Bo Schembechler. Lenny was the number-one middle linebacker on the freshman team, and I was the fullback trying to become the next Jim Brown. I tried going both ways during the early stages of that first camp. I took repetitions at linebacker in the drills, then got in line as the third- or fourth-string running back. Naturally, the only one who could tackle me when I was at running back was Lenny. A few days into that first training camp, the head coach of the varsity team, Jake Crouthamel, came to our practice and moved me from running back to middle linebacker and moved my friend Lenny to offensive guard.

Like that, he essentially took away Lenny's dream of going to the NFL. Because Lenny had the credentials. When you're All-State in high school, you think you'll go to college and knock it out of the park. Now, he's suddenly at a different position. And he's a much smaller player at offensive guard. He had to gain weight and change his body to survive in the middle of the offensive line. But the coach convinced him that was where our need was. We needed offensive linemen. Lenny put on the weight and started for two years on the varsity squad at offensive guard. But instead of Lenny becoming an enemy, an adversary, or harboring any resentment toward me for that—the switch that fueled my rise to All-America status and ultimately to the NFL—he took the complete opposite tack and became a true friend. My best friend.

He coached me up on everything he knew from playing middle linebacker. I had played outside linebacker at Flint

Southwestern, but at the next level, I became a dominant force with Lenny's help. We also pledged Alpha Phi Alpha together and became fraternity brothers. He was the guy who was right in front of me in our pledge line. I was the caboose, the last, biggest Alpha in the line, and Lenny was right in front of me. Ken Mickens was right in front of him. When I went to Mexico City during my sophomore year for the Language Study Abroad program, Lenny and I went together. When I went to the University of Southern California-San Diego the next year for psychology, Lenny went out there for sociology. After I graduated early from Dartmouth—in three and a half years, right after my senior fall football season—I stayed with Lenny at his home. His parents are like parents to me. The plan was to stay at his place then move to the YMCA in White Plains once I got a job to coincide with training in the months before the NFL Draft. The only job I got was as the assistant wrestling coach and hall monitor…at Lenny's old high school. Then I moved into the YMCA, and that's where I stayed until the draft. We were that close.

But it wasn't just Lenny and me. Grayland Crisp was with us every step of the way. The three of us were always together during the Dartmouth years—even after Gray left the football team. Gray was always very religious and ultimately became an educator. He also had a big enough influence on Lenny that when Lenny graduated from Dartmouth, he went to seminary school and became a preacher. Lenny wound up leading a church in Akron, Ohio.

By the early '90s, Lenny—whom I'd never even seen with a girl the whole time we were together at Dartmouth—now had a wife and two young children, a boy and a girl. And I guess what happened was, he found out that she was going to leave him and their two kids, and he went into the garage, started the car, and committed suicide.

That devastated me.

Why didn't he call me? If he had troubles, why didn't my best friend call me?

It was several weeks before I even found out about Lenny's death. At the time, in 1996, I was in the midst of a professional whirlwind, knee-deep into building the business at Disney that became the Wide World of Sports Complex. Although I was still in touch with him, it wasn't like we were in constant touch. But I figured if anything big was happening, we would talk.

I didn't go to Lenny's funeral because...I just didn't know what happened. I guess it was kind of hush-hush in the beginning because of the circumstances. His sister didn't even call to tell me. When I found out from one of our frat brothers, probably Fairfax Hackley III, I couldn't fathom the idea that Lenny had committed suicide. I said, "No, he didn't." It took several weeks, maybe even months, before I started accepting the inevitability that my best friend had passed away. So I called Gray.

I was like, "Gray, where *were* you?" And Gray was like, "Where were *you*?" That was rather accusatory, I know. But I felt a little bit of guilt because Lenny's life changed when Jake Crouthamel changed his position. His life and maybe his whole social persona would have been different if he would have been one of the first black middle linebackers in Dartmouth College history. I wondered whether the professional football career I enjoyed was one he resented a little bit, and maybe that's why he didn't call me when he was struggling. I was starting to feel some real guilt.

The last time I saw Lenny, I visited him in his home in Akron. It was at some point in the early '90s, when I was in Canton, Ohio, for an enshrinement ceremony or some other event at the Pro Football Hall of Fame. That's when I met his wife and kids. We had a good visit. I had no reason to suspect that anything was going wrong in his life.

I don't remember exactly when it was that I talked to him for the last time. The dream was so strong, it blocks out almost every memory except for the times we had at Dartmouth. I do recall, though, that it was an easy conversation, like they always were with Lenny. We talked about the Dartmouth years, and I know we talked about "the Smittys"—Ron and Don Smith—who pledged us into the fraternity. If only I'd known that would be the last time we talked.

Even now, I feel guilty of taking my best friend for granted. You get so busy, and you think your best friend is always going to be there. That I didn't stay in better touch with him is one of the biggest regrets of my life.

I certainly don't take him for granted now.

But in that period after learning of Lenny's death, I really blamed Gray because Gray's the one who influenced Lenny to go to the seminary. The assumption was that if you commit suicide and you're a preacher, you're going to hell. That's where Gray and I had a problem. We bumped heads. And suddenly, we were not buddies anymore.

Gray and I are good now, but the relationship was strained for several years.

Thankfully, Gray and I had patched up our differences by time I returned to Dartmouth for the fortieth anniversary reunion of our Class of '76. At a memorial service for classmates we had lost, I was enlisted to lead a reading, a call-and-response kind of reading of some verses from Psalms. That was supposed to be it. But when I went up onstage, I told our class president that I was going to say something about Lenny Nichols, my best friend. He didn't have a problem with it. Gray didn't go to the reunion, but I had talked to Gray the night before and told him I was going to do it. We prayed together, and he gave me some direction. That singular moment was very important.

Here's another thing about that day: The Friends of Dartmouth Football Golf Tournament was taking place. There's a big luncheon, and all of us are at the golf course. That's the last time I saw my former coach, Jake Crouthamel. Jack DeGange, the sports information director, was there too. I'm not able to play golf, so after the luncheon, everyone was going to their respective tees to play and I'm getting ready to leave because I'm going to speak at Rollins Chapel in a few hours. As I'm walking up this very, very steep hill, my shoes were breaking up. All of a sudden, half of one shoe just tore off! The glue just gave way. And when the shoe failed, it hurt my knee to the point that I could barely walk. I made it up the hill to my car, drove to the Hanover Inn, and barely hobbled into the front lobby. I went to the desk and asked for help. They got the day custodian to come up; he was initially going to physically help me to my room. When he saw what the problem was, he took my shoe, went to the hardware store, and identified the right kind of glue—which ended up being a compound they had to mix together—to fix my shoe. He came back to the hotel and glued my sole back together. I went up to my room to see if the pain would stop long enough for me to go over to Rollins Chapel. I'm about to go to the chapel to speak to God, and I am facing unique, painful adversity on my knee. The only good fortune I had was that I had a vape pen with me containing medical marijuana that had the capacity to blunt the pain.

When I got to Rollins Chapel, my knee was better but still not good. The shoe was back on, but the glue hadn't set yet. All I wanted it to do was just hold together long enough for me to speak into this mic on this altar about saving the soul of my best friend, Lenny Nichols. That's why the scales of pain—when I'm asked, "What mitigates your pain?"—a trial like this moment mitigates my pain. It's pain that I'm willing to go through. Any person, I think, would be willing to go through a future lifetime of pain if they believe they are saving the soul of their best friend.

In Rollins Chapel, I'm in front of God. This is a place on campus where Lenny and I had been before. I have pictures of me in Rollins Chapel with Lenny. But at that point, it was the setting for me to tell my classmates about the dream I'd had in the hospital. And I told them I was telling this story before God about strength and conviction over evil. I told them that I believed Lenny was in heaven. I spoke until the rafters shook. Because I was speaking to God, thanking Him for the salvation of Lenny.

There was no better gift that I could give to the class. I appreciated the rousing ovation that came after I finished speaking, but I know it wasn't for me. It was for Lenny.

David Shribman, the Pulitzer Prize-winning journalist and former classmate, was in the chapel that day. He called it "an unforgettable eulogy."

"Len was well known to us all, but he had a special relationship with, and effect on, Reggie, a man of considerable accomplishment and yet of deep sentimentality," wrote Shribman, who authored *Dartmouth Undying*," which commemorated the school's first 250 years. "It was the latter that shined through with astonishing power as Reggie's delivery both boomed and whispered, all in the service of his friend and as a haunting reminder of the fragility of life."

NIGHTMARE

As much as I appreciate the memories of Lenny, it would have been so much more devastating had I lost *both* of my main running buddies from Dartmouth. The reconciliation with Gray had to happen. That it came at a time of need feels a lot like destiny.

It came during the same month as the nightmare episode when I'd saved Lenny. Gray lives in Richmond, which I passed through while driving from my home in Orlando to New York for surgery. I drove because I wanted to have my car with me—just in case they cut my leg off and I had to retrofit the car to be able to drive with just my hands. The travel time alone is something like seventeen hours, and in this case the trip stretched out over a couple of days. Thankfully, I had some help: Pamela Landwirth.

Pamela is a very religious woman who runs Give Kids The World Village, one of my favorite charities. It was founded by her husband, Henri. After he passed, Pamela, who was previously the HR director at Walt Disney World, took it over to continue his vision. It's where kids with terminal illnesses can go as they pursue last wishes. If their wish is to see Mickey Mouse or to go to the Magic Kingdom, Give Kids The World fulfills those dreams. Kids come from all over the world. And I've seen kids who were given only weeks or months to live recover because they were so happy. It has saved lives. That's the spirit that Pamela carries.

In my situation, she decided to help me with the drive. With a knee operation pending, I really couldn't drive the whole way. She drove with me up to Washington, D.C., but then she had to fly back. I wound up driving the remainder of the trip alone, ending up at Dr. Tom Price's house in New Rochelle, just north of Manhattan.

Yet what happened along the way was significant in its own right. I called Gray and asked if he would meet me for breakfast as I was driving through Richmond. He agreed to meet me at a Cracker Barrel on the outskirts of Richmond.

It was a wonderful reconciliation. We renewed our brotherhood. Later that summer, it went even deeper. As I was primed to be inducted into the College Football Hall of Fame in South Bend, Indiana, Gray came through with a major assist.

Talk about friends being there when you need them. At that time, with the enshrinement looming, I was in full recovery mode after enduring five surgeries in six weeks. My leg was in a full cast. I was carrying around a vacuum to pull dead blood out of my knee. I had a concrete spacer inserted in the leg, so I couldn't bend my knee. And I had a PICC line. I was hanging antibiotics by gravity.

Well, Gray drove up to New York, picked me up, and drove me to South Bend. For the whole ceremony—the whole weekend. Then he drove me back to New York before heading home to Richmond. It was something so special for me, to have my brother there, the two of us reconciling.

That's the essence of true friendship—being able to count on someone when it matters most. Yet Gray and I were not alone on that journey.

Lenny was there too. Just like old times.

BOOM BOX: WHY THE LEGENDARY ERNIE BARNES WAS A FRIEND AND INSPIRATION

If you know the cover of Marvin Gaye's classic 1976 album *I Want You*, then you also know a slice of Ernie Barnes. The image was among Barnes's most famous works of art, titled "Sugar Shack," exemplifying a signature style capturing movement and elongation on the canvas like none other.

Barnes, who passed away in 2009 at the age of seventy, also happened to be a dear friend.

What a Renaissance Man he was, all six feet three inches of him, morphing from a professional football player into one of the most accomplished artists of his era.

His art was featured on the '70s-era TV sitcom *Good Times* (fictionalized as the work of the "J. J." character), but there was so much more. He was the official artist for the 1984 Summer Olympics in Los Angeles. He can be found in the Congressional Record, recognized as an inspiration by John Conyers. The National Basketball Association used him for a fiftieth-anniversary piece. His work is displayed at the Pro Football Hall of Fame. And on and on.

He put love and soul into every stroke of his brush.

This had to seem destined during his years with the Denver Broncos when they called him "Big Rembrandt," as he was repeatedly fined for sketching during team meetings.

I saw myself in Ernie Barnes. That's one reason we became close. If I had never played football, it's quite possible that I would have become an artist. I would have been a bohemian like Ernie Barnes. My appreciation of art goes way back, undoubtedly inspired by my Uncle Mando, a commercial artist.

You can imagine how thrilled I was to meet Barnes during my rookie year. The meeting was arranged while the Bengals were in San Diego for a game. We had about four hours before the mandatory Saturday night team dinner when a Dartmouth pal who knew Barnes picked me up at the hotel to make the hour-and-a-half drive to Los Angeles for a quick visit.

I spent less than ten minutes with Barnes that day. Basically, I just told him the reason he was my favorite artist. I explained that I was not a fan of J. J., but the TV character's redeeming value was the art. I also told him how inspirational it was for a hearing-impaired, African-American to see images that spoke to me on TV. Add the fact that he was a former player and that I still felt art was my calling, well, Barnes was a hero. We immediately became good friends. We would talk art, and I always wondered as we talked art: "What does he see differently as an artist?"

When I could afford it, I bought my first piece of art from him. If you come into my home at this moment, you'd see that set of lithographs. I added many more over the ensuing years, including "study" pieces that provided the foundation for his finished works.

The study piece for "Sugar Shack" is so valuable to me. It starts with the girl in the yellow dress. She's the focus. With that ass! He built the other characters around her. That was what he wanted. I also have Ernie's only nude painting. And one of my favorites is the study of Sylvester Stallone for *Rocky*.

Ernie lost his leg before dying of a rare blood disorder—myeloid leukemia. The first attempt to try to save his life was to cut off his leg. Given the issues I've endured, that hit home. But ultimately, his amputation wasn't sufficient to stop the blood disorder. I saw a person waste away before my eyes.

I was one of the last people outside of his immediate family to see Ernie. I visited him and his wife, Bernie, at their home in LA. And I took some marijuana for Ernie. For our whole relationship, we'd never smoked together. But when I was trying to think of the right words to tell him I'd brought something that could help with the pain, I just blurted it out, "Here's what I brought you, man." He said, "Thank you, man! That's exactly what I need!" And then we had our best conversation ever.

CHAPTER 2
RESILIENCE

Julia Williams loves to joke about the time she cried at the doctor's office. Julia is my mom, an angel of a woman who was married to my father, Eli, for sixty-six years until his passing in 2018. Their devotion to each other—and to their three sons—was an amazing model of love and commitment.

Yet at one point, my mother actually wondered whether she was an unfit parent. The notion is laughable, now as it was then, given the values my parents instilled in us and the care and attention they showered us with as they raised a family in Flint, Michigan.

Still, with an injured kid in tow again (probably me, but maybe one of my brothers), she mused that she'd wind up behind bars.

"For what?" the doctor asked.

Mom: "Every time I turn around, I'm bringing the kids to you or taking them to the hospital for some kind of injury."

The doctor calmed her nerves with his final assessment.

"Well, you have three healthy, normal boys," he said. "What do you expect?"

RESILIENCE

Injuries happened, especially to me and my older brother, Greg—born exactly eleven months to the day before I came into the world on September 19, 1954, at Flint Osteopathic Hospital—and then continued through the years with my younger sibling, Kenny.

As it turned out, the nicks, bruises, stitches, fractures, and other assorted calamities that I survived in Flint turned out to be quite the precursor of the injuries I sustained during fourteen seasons in the NFL and of the various physical challenges I've faced in my post-football years. They also formulated, in no small measure, the foundation for the resilience that has defined me like an ultimate calling card at so many turns in life.

A quick inventory:

My first fractured bone came when I was about two. I broke my arm when I fell down the steps carrying a rocking-horse toy. I vaguely remember this, but there's proof: I've got a picture of me with the cast.

There was also the time I dislocated Greg's shoulder. This was before we began going to school. He was around four years old, and I was the natural grappler who routinely tussled with him until that accident—and until the whipping our father gave us for fighting. He didn't know that Greg's shoulder had been dislocated. But after the whipping, well, Dad knew he was *really* hurt. My father regretted the spanking a little. The memory also drives home my father's adage: Learn from the mistakes of others because you won't live long enough to make them all yourself. It was an ode to my brother Greg. Learn from his mistakes. You don't want to take a whipping like he did. No, I didn't get nearly as many spankings growing up as Greg did.

My first concussion? That happened when I fell out of a tree in the park across the street from our house the summer before ninth grade. I knocked myself completely out, trying to show off to my brother Kenny and his friends. I did exactly what my mom told me not to do anymore, and I climbed to my highest point ever until...the branch broke. As I leaned forward to grab it, I saw the branch whiz past my eyes. I fell quickly headfirst and landed on my forehead. I remember coming to, with dirt flying into my nostrils. As I'm trying to clear my vision, and Kenny is saying, "Mom told you not to climb the tree!" I just got up and said I needed to go to sleep. I walked home, right across the street, where my mother was washing dishes. I just said, "Hi, Mom!" and planned to go right to bed. She took one look at me and said, "Boy, what did you do?" She grabbed me, put me in the car, and took me right to the hospital. So much for playing football during my final year at Whittier Junior High School. It took the longest time for that contusion to heal. It was way too big to put a helmet on. The swelling didn't go down for the rest of that season. That's why I didn't play football in the ninth grade.

What else? You can't see the scar on my chin because of my beard. But it's there. I was riding a bike and the sidewalk ended. I went over the handlebars and landed right on my chin. That was about ten stitches.

Years later, I had another situation with my father that I consider a demonstration of love and trust unlike any other. I was working at Hurley Hospital—one of my first jobs—back in tenth grade. While doing custodial work with another person, we dropped this heavy trunk on my toe. By the time I got home, I had this big, black bruise pulsating under the nail on the big toe of my right foot. My father looked at it and said he could fix it rather than sending me to the hospital. He went to the stove, turned the flame all the way up, got a long nail, and then he put the edge of the nail in the fire until it got red hot.

Then he got a hammer, came over, poked a hole in my toenail, and let all the blood out. Now when he told me to put my leg up there, it was total trust. This was what he'd grown up doing. As soon as he tapped it and all that blood came out, it started feeling so much better. It was absolutely the right thing to do. And after it bled out, I had this hole in my nail for about a month. So, as it healed, I was always revisiting that moment of trust. And love.

Of all the cases, there's a special distinction for getting hit by a car on the way to kindergarten: It's the only time I've ever seen my mother run. It was all my fault. We were living on the North Side of Flint, and I walked to Parkland Elementary School, as Greg had done successfully the whole year before. Well, Greg went down the street to pick up one of his friends that he always walked to school with. And as they were walking back, for some reason I imagined they were playing a game of tag, and I took off and ran into the street. Fortunately, I didn't hit the front of the car. I hit the side of the car. It just knocked me back. I'm lying on the ground, and someone ran and told my mom I had been hit by a car. She rushed to the scene. And she was hauling! It was the last—and first—time I saw her reveal her speed.

Soon after that, we moved to the South Side, to 2026 McPhail Street. My mom and dad lived in that single-level, ranch-style house for the rest of their lives. When I got my signing bonus from the Bengals, I spent nearly all of it to pay off the house. Then I bought a car. A used car. That's all I could afford with what was left. But I was so proud, and my father was so appreciative. And it was such a gift for me to be able to do that, because he had worked three jobs to get me through college—he not only worked a full shift at Fisher Body, he also did real estate and drove a cab.

I was six when we settled on McPhail Street, one of three streets in a new subdivision that sold homes to black people in 1960. A couple of blocks away, once you crossed Dort Highway, there was nothing but white people. But the kids from my neighborhood were the first students to integrate into an elementary school in Flint—Scott Elementary School—as the district included the three newest streets that had been built.

I had a great elementary school experience. The school is still there. It's now functioning as office space. But every time I go past it, I remember that's where I was when President John F. Kennedy was assassinated in November of 1963. I was standing outside the school, waiting for my mom to pick us up, and that was the first thing she told us.

I was nine. It was unsettling because the institutional confidence in the strength of your government from a personage standpoint is the president of the United States. For him to be assassinated—are we not living in primitive times? Even as a kid, that's what was on my mind. It was a fear of humanity. It started to become a fear of growing up. All kids would have loved to grow up to be the president of the United States. But to see that person assassinated? What dreams am I supposed to have as a kid?

Just as devastating, a few months before the Kennedy tragedy, four little girls perished in the church bombing in Birmingham, Alabama. They were around the same age as I was. That was a time when we'd go to church and Sunday school every week, right down the street at Quinn Chapel AME Church. I was an altar boy. I remember we were walking down the aisle, singing, "Onward Christian Soldiers, marching as to war." When the four little girls were killed, I could imagine that happening to me. They were all in the basement where bible study and Sunday school were. It was the same at my church.

It was a horror story. To have the murder of four little girls, then the assassination of the president of the United States...I just felt deflated and vulnerable as a black youth in America.

The years at Scott Elementary were also critical in dealing with another type of discovery. I was born hearing impaired, which is why to this day I have what you'd consider a slight speech impediment. As an infant, I had several medical procedures on my ear, including an experimental X-ray treatment when I was two or three years old. My mother discovered my condition after we got our first television, and I wouldn't respond to her or my father. She soon realized that I wasn't tuning them out; I wasn't hearing them.

My condition improved dramatically with treatment, and after I began school, I took speech therapy classes at the Michigan School for the Deaf, which, thankfully, was located in Flint within a few miles of 2026 McPhail Street. For a couple of years, I went there three times a week after school or on Saturdays for the specialized classes.

If you don't hear sounds properly, you can develop a speech impediment because you can't repeat those sounds, which is what I had been trying to do. Ultimately, Michigan School for the Deaf taught me mostly to cope and to understand and to control what little I could control. If I really want to hear people, I've got to be very visual. I had to learn how to read lips and read emotions. In some respects, the approach is to listen first and talk second. That's not a bad way to grow up.

Then there was Miss Chapel, my third-grade teacher. What an advocate and believer she was in me. She helped immensely, bringing an awareness to the academic environment. At first, I sat in the back of the class because we were arranged alphabetically. She walked around the room talking and noticed that when she got to the back of the room, I perked up and became really responsive. When she got to the front of the room, she looked back and saw that I wasn't focusing on her as much because I couldn't hear her. So she moved me up to the front (and I then ended up in the front in most of my other classes), and my academics improved dramatically.

I have all these memories, but it's not like the hearing issues were a major imprint on my life. The speech therapy basically stabilized me so that my lisp didn't get any worse. I also stuttered because there were some words I couldn't say, but I got that resolved. I could say most words, just not all. I don't stutter any more. I made the decision not to have hearing aids, and I made the decision not to learn sign language, which I regret.

To me, Flint was simply "Buick City" as I grew up. That's what they called the huge manufacturing complex on the northeast part of town that dominated the city's economy. That auto plant no longer exists—the auto industry's impact on Flint's decline, much like that of Detroit, the "Motor City" roughly seventy miles to the southeast, is well-chronicled— but for years it was the largest plant in the country. That made Flint a very prosperous city as I was growing up, with a population of around 200,000 in the 1960s and '70s.

So much happened to Flint during the time I played for the Bengals. Obviously, General Motors closing a lot of the plants really changed the culture. Now, as the city tries to revitalize, the population is less than 100,000, and the water crisis which affected some of the poorer communities in the city provided another challenge.

Flint had a rich cultural community when I was growing up, which continues to this day. The Mott Foundation was well-known and well-integrated culturally, providing all manner of assistance, including an extensive scholarship program and support for numerous fine arts programs. As I reflect on it,

I realize the Mott Foundation was the first corporate citizen I knew. Maybe that's why I love Mott's applesauce to this day.

We had a lot of exhibits at the Flint Institute of Arts, and we had a great library just behind Central High School, which my mom took me to every Saturday. This was an important aspect of one of the pillar principles in our household: education.

A striking memory from my childhood is that of my mother and father, sitting at the table reading and studying with me and my brothers, and not merely to help us with our homework. They were studying to earn their high school diplomas.

My mother, who was sixteen when she married my father, was a stay-at-home mom as we grew up. She eventually earned a college degree and taught special needs kids at Southwestern High. She made quite a mark in her career and was ultimately recognized as the best in the state.

My dad abruptly moved to Flint from Birmingham as a teenager after a racially charged incident on his job left him with virtually no alternative. He immediately found work in an automobile plant, the priority undoubtedly being the ability to make a living. He knew the value of education, especially in the context of what was denied in the separate-but-unequal Jim Crow system of the racist South. With that, he remained determined to ultimately resume his education and was steadfast in his demand that his three sons achieve academic excellence. He and my mom were great examples for the high standards that were set in our household.

I was always an engaged student. I loved to read, which in retrospect was predictable after an IQ test I'd taken before I began school concluded that I had an advanced learning curve. From my earliest memory, I always planned to go to the University of Michigan. It was just the logical thing. I knew what I needed to do academically to get a full ride, with my diligence lessening the financial burden on my parents. That's why U of M, under those conditions, was the lifelong dream. Winding up at Dartmouth, an Ivy League school, was some kind of destiny.

My younger brother, Kenny, lapped all of us with his academic achievements. While my brother Greg graduated from Western Michigan—my father took a third job driving a taxi to foot the bill for two kids in college simultaneously—Kenny advanced to earn his Ph.D. from the LBJ School of Public Affairs at the University of Texas. He became a professor at Michigan State and survived long enough to become tenured.

My father undoubtedly could envision our academic success. When we got to high school, he always insisted that we were enrolled in the college preparatory curriculum, which ruffled some feathers. What was unusual about how things were at that time was that one of the racial societal control valves was, "Yeah, we'll let you in our school, but we're going to teach you something different than we're going to teach our sons and daughters." So you had general classes, you had remedial classes, and then you had a college preparatory curriculum. My parents fought to get me in that curriculum. It wasn't a matter of just going to an integrated school; getting access to the best classes was just as important.

From the beginning, there were always just three black kids in those college preparatory classes. We all sat one behind the other, because of our names. It was all alphabetical. It was Lisa Weaver, Debbie Williams, and Reggie Williams. (Lisa Weaver's little brother is Wrex Weaver, who is married to Karen Weaver, the mayor of Flint from 2015 to 2019. Small world.) Lisa and her older sister Lynn—they were both varsity cheerleaders at Flint Southwestern—came to my father's funeral. It was nice of them to show up.

Being academically inclined surely put me on the proper path, but it didn't always prevent me from encountering the perils that can exist in a world where others are not so inclined. Like most places, Flint had its share of thugs, bullies, and malcontents. Ironically, my academic prowess once put me squarely in the sights of some kids who were up to no good.

In other words, I was robbed. When I attended Whittier Junior High, I was recognized for my academics, and one of the rewards was that you'd be trusted to take the money—the milk money, lunch money, or whatever—from Whittier over to Central High School, which was next door. It was a relatively short walk. Well, the one and only time I did it, some truants from the high school, two black kids, came up to me and said, "Give me the money." They knew the rhythm and that I was just another new, young kid. I gave them the money. And then all I could do was cry. I went back to my school and into the principal's office, crying. The police caught 'em, and I had to go to juvenile court to identify them. That was traumatic as hell, being a rat. But it was something I had to do.

Looking back, I guess I could've tried to fight them. They didn't have any weapons. They were just two big, strong-arm dudes. Then again, I'm not going to fight for someone else's money. But even then—it's amazing, as pugilistic as I was in my NFL days—I never got into a fight with anyone other than my brother. Just think of how my baseball "career" ended. When I was in eighth grade, I went out for the ninth-grade baseball team. My brother was in ninth grade and also went out for the team. Greg was a better baseball player. He was a big, long-ball hitter. But for some reason, when the final cuts came, they cut my brother and kept me. I had to quit the team because I was not about to walk home alone without his protection. My brother was a good fighter. The only better fist-fighter was my best friend, Ricky Taylor. "Stick" was the man. His nickname was a reflection of a stick whapping against something, like *Pow!* Early on, he had this devastating punch. We became especially close. At the same time I couldn't play football after falling out of the tree, he had a major procedure done on his hips and was in a body cast. He couldn't play either. We lived on the same block. I'd walk down and see Stick while everyone else was practicing football. I'd see him every day.

I imagine that other perilous situations were prevented, thanks to Uncle Otis. All but one of my father's ten siblings migrated to Flint from Alabama, and he was my favorite uncle. It was probably because he was the neighborhood barber. Everyone who got their hair cut on the South Side of Flint would go to Uncle Otis. His son, Otis Jr., is a barber too. It's a family business, and they cut hair out of a house converted into a barbershop.

Well, Uncle Otis heard every story out there from all the other kids. If I had to watch out for something, he'd tell me. Or he'd brag on me, which is basically protecting me, like, "Don't mess with my nephew." We had protection that we didn't really pay for and probably only deserved because of the family love. But we weren't troublemakers. None of us were. And we never took advantage of not being bullied. But there was a bit of an attitude in Flint that if you were a good-looking young man, you were more at risk for getting your butt kicked. I was so sensitive to that. Not that I thought I was a good-looking kid, but at one point I felt compelled to scar myself. The cut wasn't deep enough to get me stitches, but it was enough to give me a Sergeant Fury—he was my favorite character in Marvel comic books—kind of persona.

Of course, it was ultimately athletic prowess that helped me make a name for myself and led to a place in the Flint

Sports Hall of Fame. But football wasn't my only sport. During my last year at Flint Southwestern—and later for a season at Dartmouth—I wrestled.

I loved playing basketball, but there was a big differentiation in skills between the guys who had driveway hoops growing up and those who didn't. And we didn't. When I got to high school, I wasn't good enough to even try out for the basketball team. But finally, I decided to go out for wrestling. I wrestled as a heavyweight, so I wouldn't have to lose weight for football. But I was just barely making the minimum weight for heavyweight, which is about 205 pounds. So I was in that 205-pound ballpark.

Still, I was a force. I was stronger than I looked. My signature move was a double-leg takedown, where I was basically tackling someone. I was strong enough to pick them up and turn them over. Or, it was the move that became my rushing move as a blitzing linebacker, where you take either elbow and move the person and control their blind shoulder. Once you control their blind shoulder, you can control the leg nearest to it. Later, as a linebacker, I would control that shoulder and pull the shoulder pad so the guy lost the ability to block me from the outside. Then I'd just swing around the outside, and I'd be by him like that. It's the same thing in wrestling—you'd be able to slide behind the wrestler and, before he knew it, pick him up and put him down. As he tried to get back to all fours to get up, that's when I was waiting to do my "arm under." That was my top pin move: I'd stick my arm under his arm and up over his shoulder, then twist him over. It was a great move, very effective. I pinned a lot of opponents that way.

The defending city champion was from Central: "Big" George Washington. He was a defensive lineman who wound up getting a scholarship to the University of Minnesota and winning the Big Ten heavyweight wrestling title. He was the stud of all the heavyweights in our city and region. And I had to face him in a dual meet at Southwestern.

Meanwhile, the girl I was enthralled with also went to Central: Delores Crawford. She was classmates with Big George, and we were in the same Jack and Jill club. Her parents were light-skinned professionals, which was kind of a thing with Jack and Jill. My mom was light-skinned. Delores looked like my mom did when she was her age. I had asked her to the prom, but she hadn't given me an answer. She came to the match, where George and I went back and forth and wrestled to a 12–12 tie. It was a classic meet. I was totally exhausted when it was over. I was sitting in a chair after the match, and Delores came down from the stands and said, "Yes, I will go with you to prom." I was so excited! I didn't lose another match in the city. Then we went to the city championship.

George and I were on opposite sides of the bracket, on a collision course to meet in the final. The gymnasium was packed in high anticipation of this match. Local TV station cameras were there. When George and I first entangled, I tried a new move with him, the "suplex," where you'd try to flip a guy on his back, but I slipped. Instead, George did it to me. It was the first time I had ever been on my back on the mat. And as I looked up, I said to myself, "Wow, there are lights up in the ceiling." But that absent-minded thought lasted a split-second. All of a sudden, I heard, "You're pinned." I was devastated. And half of the audience was cheering—his crew. I was still stunned, lying on the mat, when Delores walked over to me and declared, "I'm not going to the prom with you now." She dumped me on the wrestling mat, and the TV cameras caught it! They ran it on that night's news, so I was totally embarrassed.

Delores wound up going to the prom with me anyway. I faced George again in the regional finals on the road to the state tournament. The regionals were held at a remote location nowhere near Flint. Neither of us had any fans there. I beat him, 13–6. It wasn't dramatic, but the fact that I sent him back to his high school with a loss while I was going to state was when Delores reconsidered about the prom. I should have said, "Screw you, woman." But I was so happy that she was going to prom with me. I was enthralled with her at the time.

When I made it to the NFL, I contacted Delores to come and check me out, but she had completely changed by then. We were no match.

My senior year was also the time when I made major strides on the football field. My junior year, I started at guard, while my friend Ricky Taylor was a starting defensive end. The summer before my senior year, Ricky and I really worked out hard. We either walked or ran several miles to the summer workouts every day. Every time I go back to Flint, I can't believe that I used to walk that distance, all the way from home. But that was before I had a car, and that was the only way we were going to get there. We got into the best shape of our lives. I had a great senior year. Ricky had a great senior year. Ricky and another teammate, Melford Edwards, both got scholarships to Miami of Ohio. Their team, which included Sherman Smith, who would go on to play for the Seahawks and Chargers, put Miami of Ohio on the map. That was Ricky Taylor.

I thought I was headed to Ann Arbor. I landed a full academic ride to attend the University of Michigan, and in my life's pursuit, I was going to become a doctor. All I dreamed about at that time was running onto the field at Michigan Stadium, "the Big House." I had no delusions about being a great college football player. I had no illusions about my talent.

But Bo Schembechler, Michigan's head coach at the time, shattered that dream. Not long after my senior season, he came to Southwestern and told me, to my face, that I wasn't good enough to play at Michigan. And my head coach, Dar Christianson—angling to lay the tracks for Ricky Leach, the quarterback who was two years behind me, to wind up at Michigan—was right there and didn't defend me. I was so insulted.

I still could have gone to Michigan, but not to play football. Really?

I was left with two options: One, I had a full academic ride to Albion College, a Division III school in Albion, Michigan. Or two, Dartmouth. But the Ivy League doesn't have athletic scholarships. I went home and told my dad what Bo Schembechler had said, and my father, in his own way, said, "Forget Bo Schembechler! I will pay for you to go to Dartmouth College."

He got a third job. Greg was a freshman at Western Michigan, and my father was paying for his education as well. I got some grants-in-aid and stuff, but my father was going to pay three or four times for Dartmouth what he was paying for my older brother's education. It was such a gift of parental love to know he was willing to sacrifice for me. That's why I wasn't going to let him down. And why I had such a chip on my shoulder.

Dartmouth, this determined Flintstone was coming your way. And no one cried about it.

BOOM BOX: THE REGGIE WILLIAMS BUCKET LIST

Sing a top R&B song. The band would begin with my friend Bootsy Collins, playing his star-shaped bass guitar. I'd bring something to the table too, given the experience of singing with Midnight Star and teammates

Isaac Curtis and Archie Griffin for a 1982 disco-funk record, "Bengals #1."

Create a lifetime piece of painted art. I have not yet created with my hands what my mind is conceptualizing.

Travel the world. I've already traveled half the world. I've visited every continent. Africa was a big one. But there are some places that are no longer on my list. Like Amsterdam. I always wanted to go to have a smoking vacation. But now I can have a seat here in Sarasota. Who would have thought? I'm doing it and it's legal.

Live as long as my father did. That looks to be impossible. The way I'm trekking now, living to eighty-six years old would be quite an accomplishment.

See the Bengals win a Super Bowl. Can't stop rooting—and dreaming—for my former team after all that I invested in that franchise.

Be regarded as the best player at my position in team history. I think I've done that. But it's out of my hands now. I've done all I can do to make that happen. Maybe it depends on whether someone else can come along and top me.

Induction into the Pro Football Hall of Fame as a humanitarian. This might be impossible unless the Hall of Fame establishes a new honor for lifetime achievement for community service.

Clean water for Flint. My hometown remains in my heart.

World peace. The closest to it in my lifetime was the brief moment after Obama was elected.

Fall in love again. That's a heck of a challenge. But you know what? I'm going to keep looking for you.

CHAPTER 3
ADAPTABILITY

FIRST DAY AT DARTMOUTH. I DIDN'T KNOW A SOUL THERE. There was no one there from Flint, Michigan, except me, 700 miles away from home. As promised, it was a new world. Certainly, there were no auto assembly plants in Hanover, New Hampshire, a small, rural college town nestled along the Connecticut River. And it was extremely white.

I stood on a corner in the little downtown area and was amazed watching people cross the street. It was a simple-but-cute first impression of a custom I didn't see in my urban hometown: All the cars stopped to allow pedestrians to cross the street. I had to try this for myself.

One problem: I walked, but the oncoming car didn't stop. I jumped back in the nick of time, but the car clipped me and knocked me to the ground. The old denim bib overalls that I wore—they were the "in" thing back then, patched up with little studs—were ruined. The blow from the car tore the front of the bib off. It was that close. Adding insult to injury, the car kept going.

ADAPTABILITY

It was a hit-and-run. And no one came out to the street to help me—the only brother as far as I could see. I got up, brushed myself off, and concluded: Maybe cars *won't* stop. At least not for a person who looks like me.

It was quite the welcome to Dartmouth College, the smallest institution in the Ivy League, with about 6,000 students. One of the oldest universities in the nation, it was supposedly founded in 1769 to educate Native Americans in Christian theology and English culture. But during Dartmouth's first 200 years, only nineteen American Indian students graduated.

When I arrived in the fall of 1972, though, significant changes were underway. When I accepted my admission, I didn't realize it was an all-male school! But the timing was good because my freshman year was the first time Dartmouth admitted women. With such a low percentage of women on campus—and twenty-nine black women—I felt fortunate to strike up a romance with Karen Turner, absolutely the most attractive of any of the freshman sisters.

That was also the year Dartmouth changed its team name from Indians to Big Green—just as Stanford did the same year on the other side of the country in switching from Indians to Cardinals (and ultimately to Cardinal) as a social statement. I'm supportive of the change, but my whole time there, no one had any idea what a Big Green was.

On top of that, Dartmouth aimed to diversify its student population, in part as a result of the assassination of Martin Luther King in 1968, when the admissions policies of a lot of major colleges loosened up. African-Americans became "affirmative-action" admissions. Starting in '68, Dartmouth doubled its number of black students. By my sophomore year, it had the most African-American students ever—and that number was like eighty-two.

Also, there were academic and social programs established to support Native Americans, which resulted in increased graduation numbers for that particular minority group.

Yet it was clear that not everyone was inspired by progressiveness. As I undressed at my assigned locker to get ready for my first practice with the freshman football squad, there were two white guys who refused to be in the locker room with a brother. This was 1972. They went to the equipment manager and demanded different lockers, because they didn't want to shower with any black players. Obviously, they had never played with or against black players before. They'd come from the South or some type of insulated environment. They were more prejudiced than they were great football players, okay?

When we took the field—about a hundred of us—the head coach, Jerry Berndt, announced that he was naming me as the team's captain and that I had the task of leading the squad in calisthenics. I had never done that before. I'd never been captain of any of my high school teams, but here was Berndt, setting a tone. Berndt was also the wrestling coach, and the fact that I'd wrestled in high school was also one of the reasons Dartmouth was interested in me. A few minutes before I was insulted by the rednecks, I happened to walk up as Berndt told Josh Holloway in the locker room that I was coming in with the potential to be one of the best players in school history. And suddenly I was the captain of a majority-white team. Talk about positive reinforcement. It was quite the contrast to Bo Schembechler's assessment of my potential. Coincidentally, Stu Simms (who later ran for attorney general for the state of Maryland) was the first black captain on the varsity squad that same year. As I led calisthenics, I thought about those two white boys from the locker room. In fact, I was livid.

Fate took care of it. One of the guys who refused to locker with me got thrown a pass in front of me. I hit him so hard! I had never hit anyone as hard as I hit this guy. It created such a sound, this *Boom!*, that as soon as it happened, one of my new teammates, Fairfax Hackley III, shouted, "Boomer!" I got my nickname that first day. I don't remember the name of the guy I hit, but I remember that after that hit, he couldn't play. He quit the team. My whole high school career, I'd never hit an opponent in anger. But in this case, I hit him with anger and was applauded for it. Here I was, a brother, knocking the crap out of a white guy, and everyone loved it. I knew I was in a different place with a nickname to live up to.

I was an angry black man with a chance to extract revenge against a very privileged class of people. The harder I hit them in my Dartmouth career, the more accolades I received. Ultimately, I became the first African-American All-American *linebacker* in Ivy League history. I believe I stood on the shoulders of so many great black players. It was easier for white spectators to root for a great black offensive player when they were scoring points on behalf of a team, like Calvin Hill at Yale. But there was still a reticence to watch a black guy knock out a white guy. There still was that Jack Johnson syndrome. That's what I broke through. To this day, I have the career record at Dartmouth College for unassisted tackles, and I'm number two in total tackles. The person who's number one? He played a ten-game season and played varsity as a freshman. That's sixteen more games than I played. All told, I averaged almost fifteen tackles a game and was all over the field, hurting folks.

BOOM BOX: WILLIE LANIER IS MY HERO FOR ALL THE RIGHT REASONS

Before suiting up for my first practice with the freshman team at Dartmouth, I asked for uniform number six-ty-three—Willie Lanier's number.

I wore Jim Brown's number, thirty-two, during my senior year at Flint Southwestern. But Lanier was my idol. He was my favorite linebacker, revered even more in my mind than Dick Butkus, for whom I also had tremendous respect. I identified with Lanier because he was very academic and the first African-American middle line-backer in the NFL, a star for the Kansas City Chiefs.

As fate would have it, I went through the training room asking for his number shortly after the two white guys had insulted me by declaring that they didn't want to shower and dress with black players. So me putting on number sixty-three was like Superman's S. It was like, "You guys don't know what I am going to become. You have no idea."

Lanier, a Hall of Famer, was also the first African-American and first defensive player to receive the NFL Man of the Year award for community service. It made that honor aspirational for me once I got to the point of rec-ognizing in 1982 that my career was not going to be centered around accolades as a player on the field but would revolve around the impact I had in Cincinnati. Lanier's impact in Kansas City far exceeded his great impact on the field. He was my role model.

I was sure to let Lanier know that the first time we met. It was during the mid-1980s at the Columbus Touch-down Club when I was recognized as the NFL Man of the Year. Because it was in Columbus and I'd played my whole career in Cincinnati, I was known to most of the people who came for the banquet at the hotel ballroom. But when Willie Lanier descended the stairs, no one noticed him. The conversation in the ballroom continued unabated.

I shouted above the din: "Here comes my hero! Willie Lanier! I wore his number, sixty-three, my whole career at Dartmouth College! He's the greatest linebacker of all time!"

Everyone started clapping. It was such a warm reception for Willie in Columbus.

I'm honored to follow in his footsteps. And it's no coincidence that Willie is also a signatory on the Reggie Williams Award presented annually to an inspirational football player at Dartmouth College.

My college experience wasn't just about football. And in some ways, I was hurting too. I set out to wrestle during my freshman winter term but quit after one match. Blame it on the beast that was the academic challenge greeting a pre-med major. Even though I scored mid-eighties on tests, that was C or D work. The competition was so high. I finished my first term with all Cs. I'd never worked harder academically. If I continued with my whole course load, I could probably get Cs and Bs, but that wouldn't be competitive enough to get me into medical school. I was unable to wrestle and do better academically. I had to give one up. I had to quit wrestling. Then I got sick and couldn't sleep. On the whole campus, there was not another light on anywhere as far as I could see—and that insomnia put me even further behind the curve academically.

That's when I said, in the middle of the night, "I've got to give up. I'm going to kill myself."

It was a sad option to consider, reflective of my despair. I was so depressed that I was going to let my father down that I thought of jumping out the window. Well, it was winter time, and I was on the second floor of the dormitory. The snow was so deep that if I jumped, there was no way the plunge would kill me. So I decided to jump off the bridge spanning the Connecticut River between Vermont and New Hampshire. I sprinted from my dormitory, straight down Wheelock Street, down a hill, and I was flying. Flying and crying. I was about to end it all. And it started to feel so good. I'd never run as fast. As I got close to the bridge, I figured I'd kill myself on the way back. I ran across the bridge to the "Norwich" sign and ran back. My reasons for killing myself were gone. But my reasons for continuing to do this late-night running were on. So, I changed my whole preparation. The next term, I changed all my morning classes to the afternoon so that I could run every single night. I didn't run that first football season, and I didn't run during wrestling season, but every other term I was at Dartmouth, I ran at two o'clock in the morning, like two and a half miles roundtrip. I'd run from whatever dormitory I lived in, and I'd hit that sign at Norwich. And my conditioning was always superior to anyone else's. That was one of my secret ingredients—one of the lessons I taught myself for turning a negative into a positive.

Thankfully, I overcame that personal crisis. Changing my major to psychology helped. Another factor came during spring term: I pledged a fraternity. The Theta Zeta Chapter of Alpha Phi Alpha had just been organized on campus after seven students—including Ron and Don Smith, identical twins from Seattle and bookend cornerbacks on the football team—went to Boston College every weekend for a year to earn the charter for the first African-American fraternity at Dartmouth. I was part of the first pledge class.

Dartmouth had, even to its detriment, a traditionally dominating fraternity culture. It was the inspiration for *National Lampoon's Animal House*, the classic movie co-written by Dartmouth grad Chris Miller, based partially on his experiences with Alpha Delta Phi and their zany frat house environment. The Alpha Phi Alphas, founded at Cornell in 1906, didn't have a house at Dartmouth, but we had an ideal standard that we wanted for all African-American students to survive in a competitive Ivy League environment.

Pledging was a trip. It's much different pledging a black fraternity than rushing a white frat. Our pledge line began with thirty-one students, meaning that most of the brothers on campus aspired to be an Alpha. There was no tolerance for whining. You had to grow up fast. And there was a physical toll attached to pledging. I'm sure that all of the physicality is no longer allowed, but it was different during my era. When my brother Greg pledged Alpha at Western Michigan, they broke his leg. Our thing at that time was "the Swipe"—a big paddle, big handle, hard wood on your ass. We pledged all of my freshman spring term, then finished the process early in the fall term of my sophomore year. We'd have to walk around campus in formation. I was the "caboose," the biggest guy at the end of the line. My best friend Lenny Nichols was in front of me, and in front of him was Grayland Crisp. At the front of the line was Paul Robinson, a brother from Detroit who was a nephew or cousin of Motown legend Smokey Robinson. And man, could he blow; years later, he tore it up, singing at my wedding.

We'd walk around campus wearing all black, looking like the Black Panthers. We were very intimidating. We'd walk around campus carrying bricks. And every single day we had to do "Alphathetics"—our version of calisthenics—in the middle of the Quad at the break of dawn. It was grueling. When we got to the final cut-down night, there were probably thirty of us left. And after that night, just twelve of us survived to become frat brothers. The big task that last night was to memorize and recite "Invictus," the classic poem that I'd never heard of before that night. If any of us made a mistake, someone—the person next in line behind or in some cases, all of us—got swatted. So, you had to trust the other person.

Lenny messed up right before me, which meant that I would get the blow. The look he gave me was like, "I am so sorry, Reggie." I took it with a smile and told him, "Don't worry about it, brother." Those are the things that instill a love that you are willing to go to hell for. And those were not just words I was memorizing. I was visualizing, bringing the poem to life and the situation of that moment. To me, the poem's opening phrase, "Out of the night that covers me..." meant, "Out of this room," or "Off of this campus."

I went home that summer, and even though I had yet to cross over from pledge to officially become an Alpha, my brother Greg taught me the fraternity's secret handshake. When we went to parties that summer and came across Alphas, I wouldn't get my butt kicked. I also landed a job that summer working the third shift at Fisher Body. Crazy thing: I was struck by a car, again, in a hit-and-run accident that was eerily similar to what had happened less than a year earlier on my first day at Dartmouth. Again, I was fortunate not to take a direct hit, and I walked away. I never went to a doctor for it. I basically self-treated my injury. I used the facilities at Fisher Body; they had a whirlpool and stuff. Years later, when Dr. Frank Jobe performed my first knee surgery following my fourth NFL season, he said, "You know you've had a torn ACL?" I was stunned to hear that but concluded it probably happened in that accident the summer after my freshman year.

When I returned to campus, I was still in rehab mode, unable to practice in training camp as I made the jump to varsity after being the freshman team's MVP. At least I had some help in mending: Rhea Gordon. She was a gorgeous, exotic lady from North Carolina whom I dated. Her nurturing instinct was special. I can still see myself looking out the window from my room on the first floor of New Hampshire Hall, watching her struggle with two big, heavy bags of ice for me. And I'm thinking, "I'm going to have to let her go." It shocked me. Let her go? There was an element of me saying, "I can get used to this. I can marry her. I can quit everything else and be totally satisfied with her for the rest of my life." But that threatened the focus I needed to have to get back on the football field. I knew that as long as I was with her, I'd be thinking about her.

My boys Ron and Don—they were my roommates my sophomore year—added peer pressure. They said I had to choose: the big brothers who pledged me and gave me the honor of being an Alpha, or the girl. They knew. One of my other frat brothers, Grayland Crisp, quit playing football after he met and fell in love with a woman named Lisa. After he graduated early, they got married and lived happily ever after, with two daughters who went to Dartmouth. In my case, though, I went from being in love with Rhea to being even more in love with playing football. I got wrapped up in brotherhood and teamwork. And, eventually, I was rewarded.

It was a gradual return. I didn't play at all against New Hampshire in the opener, then a few more plays in the ensuing games against Holy Cross and Pennsylvania. We were 0–3 when I made my first start at outside linebacker against Brown.

Then came a turning point: I started at middle linebacker for a showdown at Harvard.

The Crimson were undefeated (4–0), and we were the four-time defending Ivy League champs fallen on hard times. Harvard was set up to kick our ass. The 60,000-seat stadium was packed, the anticipation thick that they would finally take out Dartmouth. It turned out that we won with a monster defensive effort fueled by four goal-line stands. And for me, it was the ultimate game of my career at any level. I made over twenty tackles and must've missed three or four more. I never had twenty tackles in a game, before or since. I was all over the field, going sideline to sideline. It's the most exhausted I've ever been in a game. The only reason I had the opportunity to play in the middle was because Pat Stone—the defensive captain and a popular frat dude on campus—got hurt. Even if I had come to training camp, there was no way they were going to let me usurp his position. But I made the most of the opportunity.

The week after the Harvard game, Yale was bent to try to screw me up by going right up the middle. I responded. I was able to segue from an all-over-the-field, twenty-tackle linebacker to a ten-tackle, bust-you-up-the-sternum linebacker. The team found its groove too, as we won our final six games to claim the school's fifth consecutive Ivy League title. I went on to earn the first of three consecutive All-Ivy League honors, which was almost unheard of for a sophomore. It was just the beginning, as I would eventually become the only African-American Ivy Leaguer (after the conference was established in 1954) inducted into the College Football Hall of Fame.*

---

* I stand on the shoulders of Fritz Pollard, Brown '17 and Jerome Holland, Cornell '39, the only other two African Americans in the College Football Hall of Fame from Ivy schools, but who played before the Ivy League itself was formed in 1954.

ADAPTABILITY

That sophomore year was also when I met Harrison B. Wilson III, better known as Harry B. to everyone except me. I called him "HB Productions" because he just had a way of lighting up the room—a presence that made other people feel good. Ah, that smile. It could jump out of his football helmet. He was a year behind me, so it felt like he was my little brother. Although I had pledged Alpha and he didn't pledge, I felt closer to him than I did to many of my frat brothers. We had a unique friendship. We were both two-sport athletes, able to relate to the discipline required for that. We used to have conversations about maintaining that academic rigor. His father was president of an HBCU (historically black colleges and universities), Norfolk State, so you know he had high academic standards that ultimately led him to a successful career in law.

All these years later, when I watch his son, Russell Wilson, excelling for the Seattle Seahawks as one of the best quarterbacks in the NFL, I see so much of Harry. Russell looks and moves like his father. Harry was an exceptional athlete, a sleek receiver with great hands. He could catch the ball in traffic, catch it on the sideline, catch it when it was difficult. The ball sometimes wasn't necessarily well-thrown, but he'd go up and get it. He made a run at the NFL and spent a summer in the San Diego Chargers camp. But his legacy in the NFL is carried on so well by Russell.

It wasn't until I made All-Ivy that I started thinking about an NFL career. But the Harvard game inspired me to begin documenting my performance and outlining goals on a chart that I hung in my dorm room. I became resolved to try to understand my pro football potential as a psych major. For my senior thesis project, I came up with a model that showed how each position on the field required a different set of statistical circumstances to make a player more successful. Eventually, one can start to see the construct of an ideal player. There were several criteria beyond the physical measures. The physical dimensions give a player opportunities to play different positions, especially in the offensive line. Obviously, speed, agility, and flexibility were relevant to me, which is why I took ballet at Dartmouth. I basically created a survey and tried to come up with an answer to the question, Who is the ideal linebacker? There are psychological factors that the ideal player has to have. A linebacker has a different personality on the field than a center. Off the field, they might have similar personalities, yet their on-field personas are influenced by their positions.

Our starting center at Dartmouth, Bob Funk, was a wild man. But every one of the centers with whom I played were on the next level—and that's what the evaluation was about—like Dave Rimington, they were all laid-back, studious, totally in-control, poised people. You've got to snap the ball, so there's a different temperament required. I was looking at all these measurables to see where I fit in and how I could get to the next level. The paper wound up being printed in the *American Journal of Psychology*.

Football was just one method of expanding my horizons. The winter after my breakout season, I took off for Mexico City for the Language Study Abroad program. From the moment I arrived, it was evident that I was in for quite the education. There's nothing like immersion for learning a foreign language, which is why the program dictated that we stayed with families rather than in a dorm. Unfortunately, I didn't study my Spanish in preparation. It wasn't until I got on the plane that I wondered what I would say to my family when they picked me up at the airport. I started getting together my opening spiel: "Mi nombre es Reggie Williams. Estoy feliz de estar aquí." (My name is Reggie Williams. I'm happy to be here.) After we landed, another problem arose like the steam coming from the tarmac: I didn't have a picture or a name of the family I was staying with. As I'm walking around the airport—at least a full head taller than anyone else—I realized no one was there to pick me up. I was stranded at the airport in Mexico City without enough money to go home, and I couldn't speak the language. I decided to just listen to music and wait.

After a couple hours, I saw another Dartmouth student who hadn't been picked up. And then my fraternity brother Grayland Crisp came through the airport. The difference with Grayland was that in running to check his luggage earlier in the day, he had twisted his ankle. So not only was he stranded, he couldn't walk as his foot had swelled tremendously. I had to do something, so I picked him up and carried him over to where I had settled with my luggage (and the boom box playing music). Suddenly, our brotherhood was even stronger. We realized there must have been a miscommunication between a.m. and p.m. Someone had a phone number for the coordinator, and he eventually came to the airport and put us in taxi cabs... at about 1:00 in the morning.

The cab was a Volkswagen Beetle. The front seat was out, and it was like sitting in the backseat of a chariot. I was in Mexico City for the first time, and all of these lights shone over the sprawling metropolis. It was more overwhelming than New York City. We drove until the lights became infrequent and we entered a residential neighborhood. The driver dropped me off at the address given to him by our coordinator, a house in a quiet neighborhood. He took my luggage out, put me at the door, and left. I was stuck again. I rang the doorbell. Nothing. I rang again. Nothing. Five minutes later, nothing. Finally, after about a half-hour, I saw a light come on, and a man opened the gate. He didn't say a word or offer to help me with my luggage. He basically just gave me a nod to follow him.

This two-story house was so ornate, with such nice furniture. As I followed him up the steps, I dropped a piece of luggage. He just turned around and looked at me. He didn't say anything. I got no support. I couldn't stay there with that guy. The next morning, as I walked down the steps, a little girl about four years old came running out of the kitchen. She saw me and screamed bloody murder. She was so scared. The mother ran out of the kitchen, surely wondering what had happened to her girl. She saw me, grabbed the girl, and ran back into the kitchen. Then she ran back out with the girl, threw keys at me, and left. It was the door key. There was no way I could stay there. I didn't know where I was at, but I knew that at one o'clock I had to be at the National Museum of Anthropology— Museo Nacional de Antropología—for the first day of orientation. I had learned enough to know that I needed to take the subway.

For breakfast, the family's Indian maid cooked little tortillas and slid the plate down to me at the other end of the breakfast bar so as to stay as far away from me as possible. Ultimately, she became friendly for the week that I was there. But it was quite the chilly reception in hot and sticky Mexico.

I wound up staying someplace else, but the other place was not a family environment. They rented me a room. I was basically on my own. I didn't have any kind of guardianship. And I learned Spanish so well.

It took me just three and a half years to earn my degree from Dartmouth, but by the winter of 1975, I was eager to move on and see how well I could stack up at the next level of football. The process included demonstrating skills for the pros to assess by playing in college all-star games. I was pegged to play in two of them: the Hula Bowl in Honolulu and the Japan Bowl in Tokyo. First stop, Hawaii. I was so excited for the chance to finally play a game on national television. Remember, Ivy League competition—and exposure—was nothing like it was for the major conferences with the powerhouse football programs. No sweat. I had All-American credentials.

The defensive coordinator for the East team, George Hill, had another idea. At the time, he was the D-coordinator at Ohio State, and later he worked in a similar capacity in the NFL with the Indianapolis Colts and Miami Dolphins. When he met me, he said, "Reg, I know you were promised to be a starter here, but I had to change the defense. Instead of running a 4–3 defense, we're going to run a 5–2 defense. You're the third linebacker. You'll get a chance to play, but you're not going to get a chance to start."

As it turned out, he had two other linebackers playing defensive end. So, he had four linebackers as starters, and I'm on the bench. All week, he insulted me.

"Anyone tired? Reggie, play that position." And they would laugh.

In his mind, the Big Ten was the alpha dog of college football. And it was at that time. The Southeastern Conference wasn't as powerful as the Big Ten. My being an All-American from the Ivy League was an affront to the Big Ten, because not a single Big Ten linebacker made All-American that year.

Right before the game, in the locker room when he gave us our pep talk, Hill basically said, "These guys, these are a bunch of lazy, West Coast, surfing, beach-going players. You're going to destroy these guys! Just like they were *him*!" And he pointed at me. Everyone laughed. They were joking about me. And I didn't play the whole first half. In the third quarter, he said, "I'm putting you in the game, but only because I have to." I believe he worked it out with the opposing coach to embarrass me. They threw a little pop screen pass to Joe Washington. And I had to cover the most elusive player in college football, who just mesmerized people with his open-field running, especially on punt returns. I had to try tackling him in the open field. There was never anyone in the Ivy League who was remotely as good as Joe Washington. I went after him the first time and I missed. Aw, man! I popped up, missed again. I jumped up again, had a little bit of help, and finally hit him. I participated in an assisted tackle. He only gained a couple of yards. As it was announced who made the tackle, "Reggie Williams," Hill pulled me out of the game.

"That's why I didn't want to play you!" he screamed. And I didn't play anymore. One play. That was my only play on TV before I went to the Bengals. At that point in time, he totally destroyed my confidence. I had a better game in Japan. But on the plane from Tokyo back to New York—where I was set to prepare for the draft at the YMCA in White Plains—I seriously contemplated quitting football.

It's a good thing I had a layover in Cleveland.

CHAPTER 4
ALPHA DOGS

JUST QUIT.

That option struck me hard as I hung out at Hopkins International Airport in Cleveland during a rather long layover on the way back from Tokyo in January 1976. You would not have found me to be very good company in that moment. I was in a serious funk, my confidence still shaken by the ordeal at the Hula Bowl, when the defensive coordinator not only refused to play me but bullied me, constantly demeaning me in front of the team.

Even though I played better in the Japan Bowl, I returned home as the All-America linebacker who didn't want to play football anymore. I thought about changing my flight right there in Cleveland. Rather than continue to New York—where I would prepare for the NFL Draft—I figured I could hop on a plane to Flint, apply to grad school, and then go on to study medicine.

As I was processing this alternative plan while sitting in a remote part of the terminal, who just happened to roll down the corridor? Muhammad Ali. My hero. He was there with his wife, Veronica Porché, and his manager, Herbert Muhammad. He was just walking through. And I just had to get an autograph.

Know this: Ali was only the second person I ever asked for an autograph. The first person, Mel Farr, rudely refused to sign. That happened in the late '60s, when Farr was a running back for the Detroit Lions, and I was a ninth-grader working my first job as a caddy at Warwick Hills Golf and Country Club near Flint. After he finished a round during a Pro-Am tournament, I saw him sitting by himself on a bench under a shade tree. He had every reason to say, "Sure, kid." Instead, he insulted me. I looked around and saw another kid checking out the whole scene. I was so embarrassed. I just shrugged my shoulders and walked away. And never forgot.

Ali, though, wound up giving me more than a mere autograph. We talked for about ten minutes. I told him how my impersonation of his "Ali Shuffle" was such a hit with the other students in Mexico City. If I was bored or wanted to entertain my classmates, I'd break into the Ali Shuffle, and within seconds there would be a resounding chant from the kids, "Ali! Ali!" It was magical, and it made me feel good because I was young, I looked like him, I had a clean-shaven face, and I had my Afro cut like Ali's. I told him about that when I met him, and he got such a kick out of it.

He didn't seem bothered in the least that I had approached him. I didn't even sneak a peek at his beautiful wife, a better-looking version of my Delores Crawford. Maybe that's why he was willing to talk to me. I also told him about my state of mind: I was deflated by what had happened at the Hula Bowl… and I'd convinced myself not to play football.

He inspired me to change that thought in an instant. He convinced me to pursue my dreams, taking the time to look me in the eye and encourage me to be the football player I was capable of being.

I'm not sure why Ali was in Cleveland. This was a few months after the epic "Thrilla in Manila"—his third and final fight against Joe Frazier—when he retained his WBC and WBA heavyweight titles with a fifteenth-round TKO. His next fight was about a month away in Puerto Rico. In any event, that chance meeting was the start of a special relationship with Ali, and obviously his encouragement in that moment hit home. I boarded my plane to New York, and the next day I got a tattoo of the yin-yang symbol because of Ali. He talked to me about the yin-yang of life.

The symbol also connects to my most successful course at Dartmouth, Physics 34, for which I received a citation. That honor was so important to me because it addressed the stereotypes of being a "dumb football player" and an "affirmative-action student who could not compete academically." Well, I took one of the toughest courses offered and not only earned an A, but an A with a citation, which is so rare at Dartmouth. The course involved linking physical evidence to religious philosophies around the world, while coming up with your own philosophy...even though true faith means you really don't need any physical evidence.

When Ali spoke to me about the yin-yang, I was living proof. I went from dejected to inspired. I decided to go after the inspiration, to chase the dream. I became more determined to not look at myself through the negative viewpoints of other people. George Hill had his credibility. Bo Schembechler had his credibility. But none of them had as much credibility as Muhammad Ali.

If I had not met Ali that day, I would have quit football. It took someone on the level of Ali to completely turn around the negativity of that moment. He was an alpha dog who impacted my personal history. And it was so fitting.

I idolized Ali as a kid. I remember the night he beat Sonny Liston in 1964 to win the heavyweight title, listening to the fight on the radio while under the covers in my bedroom. But it wasn't his boxing that made Ali my hero. His braggadocious verbosity was something that a kid with a lisp, coming off a hearing issue, aspired to have for himself. And the thing that really made me love the man was when he refused induction into the military.

Vietnam represented the worst of America: being drafted and sent off to hell. All the older kids from my neighborhood who went to Vietnam came back with serious issues. Ali stood up for every neglected, disenfranchised kid who was forced to fight that war. He was reviled by much of white America, and that hatred spilled over to the treatment of black people. Yet he ultimately became respected as one of the world's greatest humanitarians. Talk about yin-yang. One of the things we chatted about was his famous commencement speech at Harvard the previous June, when he poignantly defended his positions on Vietnam and other aspects of life in America.

The other moment that still resonates was the "Ali Summit," held in Cleveland in 1967, when John Wooten called on other black athletes, including my other hero, Jim Brown, to meet and demonstrate their support for Ali. The image from their press conference—with Brown, Bill Russell, Kareem Abdul-Jabbar, Bobby Mitchell, and others with Ali—is so powerful.

When I met Ali, in Cleveland of all places, he became more than my idol.

I'm proud that we stayed in touch. I saw him at a few events during his career, and I hosted him twice for visits to Walt Disney World. The first time he came, we named a street after him.

He came back for a vacation on the property with his last wife, Lonnie, and we had dinner at the restaurant overlooking the Magic Kingdom. It was a special night.

Thinking about Ali also reminds me of my junior year at Dartmouth when I was going to quit wrestling. Again. I'd quit wrestling during my freshman year, but that had more to do with the need to drill down on my academics. The next case was a matter of will. I had this thing in my mind that somehow there could be some good to quitting, which I fortunately overcame. I never would have survived my various health challenges with such a defeatist outlook.

No, I didn't quit during what turned out to be my only full season of wrestling in college. My roommates refused to let me. I lost the first match against Harvard, and it was the only time that I gave up while competing. I had this guy beat but just didn't care about the outcome. We'd had a 3–6 football season; my mind was still on the gridiron. On that bus ride from Cambridge, which is about two and a half hours, I looked out the frost-crusted window, convincing myself to quit. I got back to my dorm and my roommates and frat brothers, Lenny Nicholls and Ken Mickens, said, "Even if you lose every match, you're the incoming captain of our football team. You cannot be a quitter. Frat brother, you will not live here if you quit. You will not be able to sleep."

I wound up winning every single match for the rest of the season and became Ivy League heavyweight champion. My championship match was against the undefeated heavyweight from Yale. The whole Yale football team was packed inside that gymnasium. Carm Cozza, the head coach, was there too. As soon as the ref hit the mat to signal "pinned," I looked up and wanted to glare. Well, Cozza had turned and wouldn't have the pleasure of getting his visual. And a lot of players had just walked out. But I became a legend at Yale.

Life will surely test the will in all of us to face adversity with determination or quit. And these tests present themselves in all types of situations.

BOOM BOX: WILLIAM "THE REFRIGERATOR" PERRY WAS THE. TOUGHEST. OPPONENT. EVER.

If you've ever run into a brick wall, then you'll understand exactly why I consider William "the Refrigerator" Perry the toughest opponent I ever encountered on a football field.

It's all physics.

Perry was the humongous defensive tackle the Chicago Bears used as a fullback in goal-line situations when they visited Riverfront Stadium early in the 1986 season as defending Super Bowl champs. He was more than a mere novelty act. Bears coach Mike Ditka crafted a special role for Perry to clear out room as a blocker or carry the football on straight-up power plays.

I was the 235-pound linebacker expected to neutralize this force.

He was *listed* at 350 pounds, but you know on Sundays, that boy was bigger.

I felt the effects of that rather quickly during a long day against the Bears. It began with Boomer Esiason throwing an interception on our very first offensive play, setting them up on our 2-yard line. We started the game in our goal-line defense with the chance to see how well our special plan to deal with Perry would measure up.

That week of practice, we watched fifteen to twenty plays on film where "the Fridge"–whose touchdown in Super Bowl XX had fueled controversy because he punched the ball in, while the great Walter Payton never scored in that blowout victory–just destroyed fifteen or twenty middle linebackers. It was such a highlight film of utter destruction that our defensive room was stark quiet. Then Dick LeBeau told us we'd counter that with what he called our "Reggie Defense."

The whole goal was for me to sneak up to the line of scrimmage at the last second, shoot the gap, and hit the Fridge low before he could get out of his stance. When they described the plan in the meeting and we had to go out and practice it, my teammates were like, "Reggie's going to be doing this? Whew!" They also looked at me like I was doomed.

Obviously, the game started with this. It was first-and-goal. The first play, it worked perfectly. I popped through the line and hit the Fridge just as he came out of his stance. *Boom!* It was like hitting a big rock. But he went down. It created a pileup and Payton fell short of the end zone. Second-and-goal. Dick LeBeau called the same defense. But now they were waiting for me. *Bam!* It was a similar collision, but they scored anyway as quarterback Jim McMahon knifed in.

Perry was so pissed after that first play, he was looking to do damage. He was waiting when we crashed into one another, and he grunted as he pounded me. Because I wrestled, I knew I could get him down. Turns out we both did.

Boomer threw another interception on his next pass, then another. His third pick on his first four throws led to another goal-line situation. It took the Bears several plays to finish that drive, ending with McMahon throwing a short TD pass to Payton. But by that point, with all the collisions with Perry in the trenches, I was pretty much through for the game. I'd never played a game where I couldn't lift both shoulders until the next day. But I had to play the rest of the game. Chicago won 44–7 and gnashed us for more than 200 yards on the ground.

John Riggins, the Hall of Famer, was the toughest pure *running back* I ever faced. He's the only running back I missed twice on open-field tackles. The second time, in Washington, he was running a wide sweep. I had him dead to rights and hit him perfectly. I tried to wrap my arms around him, but he just kept running through it. I was like, "Aw, man! *Twice?*"

Then there was Earl Campbell. The greatest compliment I ever got from a Hall of Famer came from the bruising former Houston Oilers running back. He said that the hardest hit he ever absorbed during an NFL game came from yours truly. Coming from Campbell—who probably inflicted way more punishment than he took—that assessment is like a special badge of honor.

But the Fridge still represented the greatest physical challenge of them all—with or without the ball.

Take the life-or-death scenario I found myself in while studying in Mexico as a college sophomore. This experience started at Denny's, of all places. That's where you could meet Mexican women interested in Americans. And it's where I met this older, well-to-do woman who spoke English. She invited me to go with her to see *El Maestro*. The teacher. He was a former fighter pilot, paralyzed from the neck down after his plane was shot down and his parachute didn't open. He became a spiritual leader for hundreds, if not thousands, of rural Mexicans. We drove an hour, maybe an hour and a half to see him at some unknown rural village outside of Mexico City. I was cool with the timing because my beautiful date was a captive audience.

When we got to El Maestro's place, he was sleeping. That gave me a chance to tour the grounds. His house was in the center of a garden, with his living area turned into almost a little park. They had stripped the leaves off the trees and painted them white from the trunk up. You know how eerie it is at night, in the moonlight, to see all these little branches going up into the stars? In the middle of it, they had a place to sacrifice animals. There was already a lot of blood in the cauldron. Interesting. I had a session with El Maestro. No problem.

A few weeks later, the woman and I made a return visit. After we got there, I acted as if I knew my way around. I walked around the rural village, which was all dirt roads and huts of adobe construction. I met some people from Mexico City who were also there to see El Maestro, and we decided to exchange numbers. I searched for something to write on, but the ground was so clean. There was nothing disposable. I kept walking until I saw a pile of debris. A wall enclosed the place, but I went in through an open gate. It was private property. I walked to the trash pile to get a sheet of paper, and as soon as I picked it up, out of nowhere, I saw these dogs surrounding me.

There were more than I could count. I was ready to sprint, but one of the dogs had cut off my retreat. Judging by their facial direction, I immediately knew the dog that had sent him was the alpha male. The other dogs sniffed me; they put saliva on me. I could see the see the saliva sliding off their fangs. Their ribs poked out of their sides. You could tell they were hungry. They were ravaged. The only one that looked thick was the alpha. I just stood there looking at him. I didn't have a volatile expression on my face, but my demeanor said, "I dare you. You don't know who or what I am." That type of defiant mindset. They were barking and poking their noses right up my ass and crotch, sniffing for any body fluids. If I would have defecated, they would have devoured that along with my butt producing it. They were nosing in my butt cheeks for signs of fear. It wound up being a three-hour ordeal. It was daytime when it started, and I slowly watched the dusk come and night fall. I didn't move that entire time. Eventually, the alpha dog gave me one look—he'd always had his eyes on me, waiting for me to screw up—and decided to leave. If I had done anything aggressive, he would've given them the signal to attack. There's just no way you can fight off a pack of dogs. And in three hours, no one came to help. How did I come out unscathed?

I have no idea what happened to the people from Mexico City with whom I'd exchanged phone numbers. They disappeared. The woman that I came with was in line, waiting to see El Maestro. By the time I walked back, it was my turn to see him. She was in the room with me when I had my session, and El Maestro said, "You've already had your lesson for the day." The girl said, "What does that mean?" I looked at him and said, "Si, El Maestro, si." He said, "I'll see you next time for your next lesson." I don't know what he knew or how he knew it, or whether he knew it from a spiritual standpoint or if someone had told him I was damn near killed by a pack of starving dogs. Regardless, he didn't send help. In my gut, I felt like it was his third eye. And that's the special gift for which he had a such a following. He could see life through a mind's eye. He could see problems. That's why the people came to see him. He provided protection against the future and guidance against the unknown. That was one of the most terrifying moments in my entire life and, yes, a lesson that significantly changed me. The lesson: Don't panic. Know yourself well enough to survive in the most unusual circumstances. Keep your poise.

But I didn't want to learn another lesson from that dude. I never went back.

Over the years, I've read numerous stories about people—from grown men to little children—being attacked and even killed by dogs in various situations. Cases like these may be rare, but they reinforce the reality of the danger I faced with that pack of dogs. I also can't help but believe that I was prepared for that moment in Mexico because of what I'd encountered in Flint years earlier.

When we lived on the north side of Flint, it was routine to see packs of dogs. It's why our house had a fence around it. We lived right across from the General Motors factory off Industrial. People would bring their dogs to work, and they'd lose them. That's where these stray dogs came from. People let them run free around the properties because they'd go after mice and feral cats. You definitely wanted to avoid them. People got bit by these dogs all the time. You also learned to differentiate between the pack and the alpha male. The stray dogs would lead the pack, unless the alpha sent out scouts ahead of it. The communication among a pack of dogs is amazing. Just don't run. I've seen people try to run. My brother Greg tried to run once. That dog caught him and bit him in the ass. He's probably still got those teeth marks on his butt cheek right now.

Then again, these life lessons also better prepared me for a career in the NFL, which is its own type of dog-eat-dog world.

CHAPTER 5

NEXT LEVEL

SICK. ALONE. STRESSED. THAT ESSENTIALLY SUMS UP THE "Reggie Williams NFL Draft Day Party," live from a tiny room at the YMCA in White Plains, New York, as I waited for the phone call that for a while—a long while—seemed like it would never come.

It was April 8, 1976—absolutely the longest day in my life.

This was before the draft became the made-for-TV spectacle that it is today, with cued-up highlight reels and instant analysis as each pick is announced on a grand stage.

No, there was no red carpet or green-room treatment for me. Just a guy with the flu, sicker than I had been on any day during my time at Dartmouth and, as the hours ticked off, wondering why Gil Brandt had lied to me.

Brandt, then the Dallas Cowboys' personnel director, told me that they would take me in the first round. Not quite. Dallas took a cornerback, Aaron Kyle, with the twenty-seventh pick overall. And when the Cowboys also picked twice in the second round and twice in the third round before I went off the board, they hadn't drafted Reggie Williams.

My call finally came around 5:30. Up until then, I thought I had made a serious mistake by not signing with the Canadian Football League and that I might not be drafted at all. Without the minute-by-minute draft updates we're used to today, I figured they were probably down to the fifth or sixth round when someone knocked on the door.

Back then, the YMCA had an operator and a switchboard. You had your own phone, but you couldn't dial out. The voice was urgent: "There's a phone call for you!" I'm thinking it's the NFL team that drafted me, but it's Jerry Albright, general manager of the Toronto Argonauts. He offered me another $100,000 on top of his previous $400,000 offer because the Cincinnati Bengals had just drafted me. He already knew. He got to me even before the Bengals could call me. He said, "But you've got to accept the offer now!"

At the time, that was big money. Weeks before the NFL lottery, the Argos had drafted me in the first round and rolled out the red carpet that I didn't get from the NFL. Their big star was Anthony Davis, the former Southern Cal tailback. When I visited Toronto, Davis picked me up in a Rolls-Royce and toured me around town. So, as the NFL Draft rolled on, Albright's offer was tempting, especially since I didn't know that I had already been picked; all I knew was that I was nowhere near being the first-rounder that I was led to believe I'd be. And, frankly, if I had been drafted anywhere lower than the third round, that would have messed with my ego.

While I talked with Jerry, I got another knock at the door with another message: "Someone from *Cincinnati* is trying to reach you." I told Jerry I had to go. That's when Mike Brown got on the phone and told me they had drafted me, third round, eighty-second overall. For me, it was like salvation. They had pulled me out of this morass. Sorry, Argos. There was no way

I wasn't going to play for the Bengals. I was quoted in a newspaper story back then, when asked why I'd turned down twice as much money from the CFL to play in the NFL: "Playing in the Canadian Football League is identity suicide." I said that in 1976. It's even more true now. The CFL has become totally irrelevant.

Besides, joining the Bengals came with a personal twist. Mike Brown was from Dartmouth. I didn't visit Cincinnati, or any team for that matter, during the weeks leading up to the draft. But the Bengals were represented by the BLESTO scouting combine at my pro day workout on campus, when I ran a sizzling 4.6 in the 40-yard dash at 215 pounds. Plus, Mike surely did his homework in other ways. I agreed with his assertion that he knew more about me than any decision-maker in the NFL.

What a deal. I was drafted by a Dartmouth grad. I should also point out that this was the beginning of an interesting lifetime relationship with Brown that included a multitude of twists and turns over the years. But at least we had some common ground.

Mike is the son of one of the NFL's most remarkable legends: Paul Brown. Paul's mark on the game includes revolutionizing the coaching profession, pioneering technological advances, and, as the Cleveland Browns coach in 1946, reintegrating pro football by signing Bill Willis and Marion Motley as pillars for a team that won all four All-America Football Conference championships before it merged into the NFL. Paul Brown's history undoubtedly provided Mike with quite the foundation for ultimately running the franchise that his father founded. To the surprise of many, though, Mike had played the game too. He was the starting quarterback for Dartmouth's

1956 team, setting the school record for most touchdowns with the fewest number of yards—as in a lot of quarterback sneaks.

Naturally, Mike kept tabs on Dartmouth football. And surely he insisted that if it weren't for him knowing me, no one else would draft me as high as he did.

Regardless, I came in with a huge draft class, back when the draft went on forever to the tune of seventeen rounds. I was a third-round pick and the sixth player drafted by the Bengals in 1976. They had two picks in each of the first three rounds and, over the entire draft, a total of twenty-four picks. A lot of us made the team, like eight or ten of us. Everyone drafted in front of me made the team except Danny Reece, a defensive back from Southern Cal. He wound up playing for Tampa Bay. Greg Fairchild, a guard from Tulsa, and Nebraska running back Tony Davis made the team as fourth-rounders. Melvin Morgan, a DB from Mississippi Valley State, was an eleventh-round pick who made it. Another DB, Scott Perry, made the team from Williams. And our fourteenth-round pick, Greg Coleman, didn't make our team but came out of Florida A&M to play twelve seasons in the NFL, primarily with the Minnesota Vikings, as one of the few black punters in NFL history.

In some ways, it seemed like I had to fight to make the team. Literally. Every single day during my rookie training camp, I came to blows with somebody—usually an offensive lineman I tangled with in the trenches.

But then there was Kenny Kuhn, a seventh-round linebacker who had been the captain of George Hill's defense at Ohio State. Yes, *that* George Hill. The guy who thought I was a piece of crap because I was from the Ivy League instilled that same belief in Kenny Kuhn. During my rookie camp, Kuhn picked on me every single day. But there was no way

I would take his mess. First, we got into a fight on the field. It was an example of the one thing I learned from fighting with my brother Greg, and it's why I never got into a fight with my Flintstone pal, Ricky "Stick" Taylor.

A quick flashback: He who throws the first punch usually wins the fight. Stick got his name because of that. He had long arms, and if you were in "Stick range" taunting, you'd better watch out because he would clock you and the fight would be over. Greg, before I got big enough in the tenth or eleventh grade to manhandle him, would end the fight by hitting me in the face. *Pow!* I contended that was against the rules because our father said we could beat each other up all day...if we didn't hit each other in the face. Don't disfigure each other. Well, when I got the best of Greg, he cheated.

By the time I was in the NFL, that lesson had been instilled in me. The first time Kuhn crossed the line on the football field, it was over. I hit him as hard as I could before he could get out one more smack-talking word. Some of his Ohio State team-mates were on our team. One was Archie Griffin, the Heisman Trophy winner picked in the first round. Another was quarter-back Cornelius Greene. And I'm beating up one of his other captains. No matter. We had to scrap. And you had to almost knock Kuhn out because he would keep coming at you. If people didn't hold him back, it would have been much worse for him. Then he picked on me in the lunch room. We had this full-out, no-helmet fight. I bloodied him up. Then we fought again in the dormitory one night. This dude probably went and called George Hill: "He kicked my ass. What should I do now?" And Hill probably told him he'd better go back at me the next day. He apparently didn't know I was going to beat him up and show no mercy.

(Kuhn, who never played in an NFL regular-season game, committed suicide in 2006).

If not Kuhn, it was somebody else. It was a rare day that I didn't fight someone during my rookie camp. I think we were doing three-a-days then, under Bill "Tiger" Johnson. This went on the whole six weeks. I had to prove myself. But along with most of my teammates, we never had fights during a game because that would get us thrown out.

My first game in a Bengals uniform was at Lambeau Field in Green Bay, Wisconsin, for the preseason opener against the Packers. That place is so immaculate. Right before the opening kickoff, as I was set to take the field for special teams duty, big Bob Johnson and Coy Bacon got on either side of me. They ordered: "You'd better make this first tackle!" I was more scared of them than of the entire Green Bay organization. There was not anybody who was going to stop me from making that first tackle, and I surely got in on it, combining with another player for the stop. They announced my name on the PA system on my very first play at Lambeau Field! Coming off the field, I veered off so that I'd pass the two vets who had shown such an interest in me. I expected one of them to say something like, "Way to go, rookie." They totally ignored me.

The next kickoff, I got to the pileup late, but I jumped onto it. At least I was around the ball. Then we started smelling something. There was a Packers player in those beautiful pants—white with that gold-and-green stripe down the outside—and he'd literally had feces knocked out of him. He had this oozing brown spot on his pants. We were like, "Ughh!" I'm from an Ivy League school. That's what some people expected would happen to me when competing against players from college powerhouse conferences. From that point on, I decided

I wouldn't eat anything before a game. All I'd have was liquid. Water, coffee, orange juice. I'd eat after the game.

My last meal the night before a game? Apple pie. No matter if it was at home or on the road. Worst case, I'd get apple pie à la mode at McDonald's. It was like death row: This is your last meal. Every week. Say what you want, but I never got feces knocked out of me. But I saw it and smelled it on that guy. There's nothing as bad as getting the s*** knocked out of you in front of everyone in the middle of a football field, and you've got to wipe off the brown spot. Oh my goodness. I don't remember anything else that happened in that game. As a rookie, I would have played some defensive snaps, probably in the third or fourth quarter. But I don't remember. The whole time on the sideline, I was thinking about that.

A better rookie memory came on the day of the final cuts. We had our last preseason game on a Saturday night and had to report back to the team's headquarters on Monday. You'd walk into the building and "the Turk"—which is what they called the guy who informed you to turn in your playbook because you'd been cut—was on the left. If you made it past his door, then you'd made the team. A few days before that final cut, Melvin Morgan, the eleventh-round pick from Mississippi Valley State, had made a proposition: "If I make the team," he said, "I'm going to shave my head. You want to do it with me?" I said, "Yeah, man. I'll shave my head too." Well, we made the team and got our heads shaved the next day.

I found a more significant way, though, to mark the occasion of officially becoming an NFL player. I looked in the phone book and found the Cincinnati Speech and Hearing Center. I drove there and introduced myself to the general manager, Carol Leslie. I told her I wanted to volunteer. I told her about my experience at the Michigan School for the Deaf, of how I'd benefitted from taking speech classes in college, and how much I had overcome my speech impediment. I told her I was willing to help. She embraced that and got me completely involved. I became a board member of the National Association for Hearing and Speech Action. That became my platform, and it started on the very first day I made the team. It was the first place I found on my own in Cincinnati. I did that before I even tried to find a place to live.

The football worked out too. After Kim Wood, the Bengals' renowned strength and conditioning coach, put me on a program during the offseason, I bulked up to 228 pounds and shaved my 40-yard dash time to 4.55 seconds. That helped tremendously in the transition to the next level. And I felt like Superman the way I flew around, literally hurdling blockers with reckless abandon.

I started ten games in 1976 and was named to the NFL's All-Rookie team. So there. From deemed not good enough...to one of the best new players in the league.

Right at the end of my second season, I connected with a new running partner: Endangered Species. The reason he got his name was because he was a merle—a gray Great Dane with black spots. That's a dominant strain. There was a breeder selling Harlequins—white Great Danes with black spots. But because of his color, his brothers and sisters were selling for $500, and the breeders were selling him for seventy-five bucks. And they were only selling him for extra cash because it was Christmastime. Normally, they kill merles. When I put him in the car and turned on the radio, the first song I heard was the Parliament song, "Bop Gun (Endangered Species)." I said, "Man, you've got a theme song!" I named him Endangered Species. And I trained him 100 percent in Spanish. That's the corollary to my regret for not learning sign language.

Species was phenomenally trained, but he only listened to me in Spanish That was also related to the pack of dogs I encountered in Mexico. Because when it first happened, I wanted to shout at those dogs. You want to use your voice as a weapon or communicator of danger. But anything I would have said in English, they wouldn't have understood anyway. All they knew was Spanish. And if I messed up in Spanish, I might have been telling them to kiss my ass. Or something that might sic 'em on me. So, it was better to keep my mouth shut.

Species went everywhere with me. He even got kicked out of Spinney Field, our team headquarters. I could walk from my house to Spinney Field, and I would occasionally take him with me during the offseason. But this one Tuesday during my fourth season with the Bengals, I brought him with me. It was the players' day off, and I was in the weight room. The strength coach, Kim Wood, didn't mind Species. He was very docile. Then, my linebackers' coach, Hank Bullough, pulled all the linebackers out of the weight room for some "emergency" film session on our day off. When we went into the room, Species sat right outside the door, chilling. Then Forrest Gregg—in his first year after replacing Homer Rice as head coach—walked down the hallway toward him. Once he got to a certain point and it was perceived by my dog that this guy was coming between him and the door, Species stood up and barked so loud the building shook. *Woof! Woof! Woof!* Usually, Great Danes are scrawny things, but Species had this big barrel chest. He was imposing. Forrest burst through the door shouting, "Get that [expletive] dog out of here!" He was scared as hell. I've never seen Forrest scared other than that one time. I glanced at Hank and said, "Look at what you got me into," then got up to get Species. That was his last visit to Spinney Field.

Of all the head coaches I played for with the Bengals, Forrest was my favorite. Homer Rice was my second favorite. Homer, unfortunately, couldn't command the respect of the players in the locker room. It's why his tenure was so short. But in terms of developing leaders and being innovative, he was an excellent human being. And there was a lot that I liked about Sam Wyche. But my first Bengals coach? Bill "Tiger" Johnson sure rubbed me the wrong way.

During my second training camp, I got into a fight with Bob Trumpy, the big tight end who later went on to become a big-time broadcaster. Years later, I told him about the fight, and he had forgotten about it. But I remember it to this day. And it was inspired by Tiger.

My position coach, Howard Brinker, was in the hospital. He didn't coach the linebackers in our first preseason game, which we lost. At the first practice the next week, Tiger Johnson stopped everyone after we broke up for calisthenics and made an announcement: veteran players can't lose their job due to injury. Therefore, Ron Prichard—who'd lost his job to me when his knees went out the previous year—was reinstalled as the starting right outside linebacker. And you, Reggie Williams, even though you were NFL All-Rookie, you are now on the bench. And he made this announcement at practice! He didn't talk to me beforehand. My linebacker coach wasn't there. I was so beyond pissed.

Well, that was the year (okay, *one* of the years) the NFL tried to cut down on infractions. My rookie year, you could clothesline players and you could head slap. That was Coy Bacon's weapon in '76; that's why he had all those sacks— we counted twenty-six in fourteen games. Coy came from the Rams with that head slap, but it was outlawed the next year. On my first play after Tiger Johnson demoted me, I was suddenly on the second team, going against the first-team offense and Bob Trumpy. It was a seven-on-seven drill. I lined up in front of Bob, and he came up off the snap and head-slapped me. Before he could take another step, I went into this flash of anger, and I took everything that I wanted to do to Bill "Tiger" Johnson and did it to Bob Trumpy. I quickly grabbed him by the helmet and flipped him over my knee. He landed at least 5 yards away looking up through his ear hole. Everyone laughed.

As Trumpy got up, Tiger Johnson came shouting in my face: "That's why you got demoted! Because you didn't do that Saturday night on the football field!" Out of the corner of my eye, I saw Bob coming at me. He'd taken his helmet off. He was winding up, getting ready to coldcock me while Tiger berated me. Tiger could see this, but he didn't warn me. Trumpy threw a punch. I blocked it with my left arm—that's a wrestling move—and he was wide open. I looked at his face, and I was angry because I was getting reamed out. And because his head slap was illegal. He messed with the wrong person at the wrong time. He was one of those white boys that looked down on me for being an Ivy Leaguer.

Pat McInally, the punter, had issues with his Ivy League rep too. Pat was from Harvard and couldn't play at all his rookie year because he got hit on one play in the college all-star game. They started calling him "Candle"—one blow and you're out. As a linebacker with an "enforcer" role, I was supposed to be the inverse of him. But being an Ivy Leaguer, I had to doubly prove it. And no, Pat was not allowed into the little locker room clique that basically consisted of the offensive line, plus Kenny Anderson and Bob Trumpy.

It figures that the day Bob Blackman visited practice, I treated him to a fight. Blackman was coaching at Illinois then, but before that, he made his mark in the Ivy League. He was head coach of Dartmouth's greatest team, the 1970 squad that went 9–0 and won the Lambert Trophy. I played for his successor, Jake Crouthamel, but I had much love and respect for Bob Blackman. I was thrilled that he came to one of our practices during my second year, and he was there with Paul Brown. Sure enough, I got into a fight with an offensive lineman right in front of them. Oops! Sorry.

That second NFL season was not unlike the others in that it reinforced the price that so many players pay for the opportunity to put their bodies through the "weekly car crashes" inherent to our violent and physical profession. There was a game during my second season when I was not going to be able to play because of a knee injury. It was officially "a game-time decision" in more ways than one. I was in the locker room with the trainer and Coy Bacon, the respected defensive end who had implored me to make that first tackle in my first preseason game. Now Coy was urging me to make another type of play for the team. He was opting to take the needle—a cortisone shot—to be able to play. He said, "Rookie, we need you today. You going to join me?" I took the shot. It was the first and only time in fourteen years in the NFL, because I had such a negative reaction to it. I was able to play, but I couldn't confidently play. I didn't trust the needle.

I was able to reject the constant cortisone shots that many players subjected themselves to, but, unfortunately, I can't say the same about surgery. Over the course of my NFL career and beyond, I've had twenty-seven surgeries—most, if not all, part of the price for playing the game that I loved.

The first surgery was right after the 1979 season, when my knee injury was exacerbated by Greg Pruitt's tackle after an interception in the season finale. I already had cartilage damage and was limping a bit as I went to and from the huddle. The Cleveland Browns' coaches decided to take advantage of that. They sent Pruitt, the running back, on a pass pattern where he would run to 6 to 10 yards, then break for the sideline. There was no way I could break like Greg Pruitt. He got a reception and ran 12 yards before I got an angle and, with the defensive back, got him out of bounds. Then they lined up in the same formation and ran the same play. I was pissed! That's an insult. How dare you run back-to-back plays to take advantage of me? I didn't feel the pain in my knee on the second play. I ran with Pruitt, jumped in front of him, intercepted the ball, and took off down the sideline. I was going to score. But Greg caught me and grabbed my right leg. You can see on the film that he twisted it as we were going down. My teammates helped me off the field, and my season was over. Torn cartilage.

That was the rough ending to my fourth NFL season, which ironically also left me fully vested for benefits. On the heels of that dismal 4–12 campaign, I went to Los Angeles to have the surgery at Centinela Hospital because I was trying to go to the best doctor in the world for it—Frank Jobe. Given the advances in medical technology, it's fair to suppose that my case would have resulted in a relatively minor procedure today. But back then, it was major. This was before arthroscopic surgery, so they opened up the whole knee and took out all the cartilage. The rest of my career, I played bone-on-bone inside my knee.

After surgery, I spent the whole offseason in LA. While the primary purpose was to rehab the knee, that was hardly the only omen for what was ahead.

BOOM BOX: KEN RILEY SHOULD BE IN THE HALL OF FAME

It burns me that Ken Riley doesn't have a bust in the Pro Football Hall of Fame.

Check out the NFL's all-time list for career interceptions, and my former Bengals teammate is tied for fifth with sixty-five picks. The four ahead of him (and many way lower on the list) are already enshrined in Canton.

There's no way he shouldn't be considered for the Hall. Now you're seeing safeties with only half of his interception total—like Kenny Easley and Troy Polamalu with just thirty-two each—get inducted. Brian Dawkins was elected in 2018 with thirty-seven picks.

The case for Riley, aka "the Rattler," begins with his consistency over such a long period of time. He played fifteen NFL seasons, converting from an excellent quarterback at Florida A&M to a defensive back with the Bengals, and he performed admirably from the beginning.

He played 207 regular-season games for the Bengals, which is the franchise record for non-kickers (I played 206) after joining the team in 1969 as a sixth-round pick. He still holds the club records for career interceptions, interception return yards, and touchdowns off those returns. And his nine picks in 1976 stood as the team's single-season record for thirty years.

No, Rattler never made the Pro Bowl, but that shouldn't disqualify him from the Hall. I suspect there was something systemic about the public relations effort—or lack thereof—that worked against the defensive players in Cincinnati during that era. On top of that, he was always overshadowed during his career by Lemar Parrish, who was very flashy and talkative—which Rattler is not—and Parrish also gained a lot of notoriety for his role as a punt returner. So, Lemar would be the All-Pro.

But Rattler was such a team player. I mean, I only got hit from the blind side two times in my career, and both times, it was because I didn't listen to Rattler's warning. He was also a very calming force on the field and in the huddle. I don't think he ever had an unsportsman-like penalty. He was well-respected by teammates and opponents, and had a deadly style of tackling. His nick-name was a play on FAMU's team name (Rattlers). But he kept the nickname because his tackling style was like a snake grabbing you out of the grass. He would always tear your ankles up.

Riley also happened to be the only Alpha Phi Alpha teammate I had. We were frat brothers who formed an instant bond and were both more cerebral than the typ-ical NFL player at that time. He was very academically oriented at FAMU, captain of their offense, a quarter-back, a leader on campus, and a Rhodes Scholar can-didate. That he went on to return to his alma mater to become head coach and athletic director is so fitting.

I appreciate that he always instilled confidence in me with positive reinforcement. He likes to tell the story about the first time I played against Houston and their tall receiver Kenny Burrough. This was when you could hit wide receivers all over the field. Riley told me before the game to be aggressive, and I just went wild on this wide receiver and wouldn't let him off the line of scrimmage. I was maniacal about it. He went to Rattler, because he knew him from his college days at Texas Southern, and said something like, "Hey, what's wrong with your linebacker? He's crazy, man." Riley said, "Yeah, he is crazy. I don't know what's wrong with him."

Then Riley came to the huddle and said, "Keep doing what you're doing, Reg."

Rattler had a tremendous impact as one of the game's greatest ball hawks ever, which is why I feel so strongly that he deserves a place in the Hall of Fame.

CHAPTER 6
DEMONS

THEY CALL IT THE CITY OF ANGELS, WHICH WAS RATHER appropriate since I wound up singing in a gospel choir while spending the 1980 offseason in Los Angeles rehabbing after knee surgery. The physical comeback was one thing. But I was seeking some spiritual rehab too.

That led me to join a bible study group headed by Frank Wilson, a pastor to the stars. Wilson was a writer for Smokey Robinson in Detroit. When Motown moved to California, he came too, and basically took care of the spiritual needs of many of the performers. It wasn't a typical bible study assembly. We met on Saturdays at the home of a musical legend—either at Smokey's house or that of Philip Bailey, a headliner for Earth, Wind & Fire—and the group's mission included various community outreach ministries.

Well, there was a prerequisite: You had to know how to sing to join Wilson's study group. They taught me how to hold a note by forcing me to join the choir at Mt. Zion Missionary Baptist Church. In the middle of Compton, Mt. Zion is, to this day, one of the most established black churches in the LA area.

Who'd have thought this would be my first exposure to Compton, where I would return for another mission with the NFL a few years later? At the time, the church was headed by the Reverend E. V. Hill, once named by *Time* as one of the seven most outstanding preachers in America and by *Ebony* as one of the fifteen greatest black preachers. It's also the church where then-President George H. W. Bush visited after the riots in 1992.

Yes, I was in some deep spiritual company at Mt. Zion. I never imagined, though, that association would include intimately battling the devil in a way I had only heard about.

Her name is Terri McFaddin. Her resume includes two Grammy Awards won as a songwriter at Motown, and she's written several inspirational books. Yet in the early '80s, she was one of the bible study leaders who was passionate in helping to strengthen my spiritual foundation. Ultimately, she left the music business, went to a seminary, and became a full-time minister. I can see why.

On two occasions, Terri asked me to accompany her as she performed exorcisms. Let me repeat: *exorcisms*. The first case involved a woman, a church member, in the hospital. Terri asked me to come along to be her rock—an immovable force to lean on as she sought to rid this person of evil. If she felt challenged or moved, to keep her faith, she could look to me.

I was impenetrable, with the same countenance I had when facing the dogs in Mexico. Facing the devil and staring down a pack of dogs requires the same level of focus and intensity. I looked at Terri as she worked with her patient. This wasn't the image you'd remember from the '70s-era horror film *The Exorcist*. The bed didn't jump. But it was still supernatural. I saw the woman's contortions and heard the repeated verses from Terri. There were changes in the hue and light of the room and changes in temperature. Terri was expelling this spirit: "Get thee back, Satan! Get thee back, Satan!"

I lost track of time, but the next time I was thinking my own thoughts, more than an hour had passed, and it was dark outside. Terri ultimately calmed the woman and put her to sleep. That transformation was the job we were called to make. The patient was released from the hospital the next day with surprising cessation of her symptoms.

The second one was a guy, probably two or three weeks later. I'm not sure if it took place in a hospital or a nursing home. It wasn't a private home; it was some sort of institution. I know the exorcisms were real because of the changes I saw in both people. We weren't giving anybody injections, pills, liquids, or anything. We weren't putting a lot of hands on these people, although Terri would occasionally hold firm on an afflicted area that might be quivering. But I was also seeing the resistance, the fight of the people. That's when you know there's something else there beyond just what you can see.

After the second one, it was like when El Maestro had said, "You've already had your lesson for the day." I would not do exorcisms for the rest of my life. The offseason was ending and I was about to leave California, so it was a "no thank you" on the next one. But I know how real, how serious, these situations are. You're tempting the devil and surviving a catastrophic spiritual confrontation with each one.

Reflecting on them now, those experiences fortified me for the encounter I would have years later when I went to hell through a nightmare to save the soul of my dear friend Lenny Nichols.

When I returned to Cincinnati, the Bengals were transitioning to our third head coach in five years, Forrest Gregg. I remember introducing myself the first time he walked into the locker room. He towered over everything when he came through the door. Even as a retired player—he'd made his mark as an anchor tackle for the great Green Bay Packers teams under Vince Lombardi—he was an immense person. That leaves you immediately intimidated, which was exactly the ingredient we needed. He didn't spend much time on the defense. He left that responsibility to Hank Bullough. Forrest only spoke to the defense when we did something really bad… or really good. I was saddened when he passed away in 2019.

After back-to-back 4–12 finishes under Homer Rice and Tiger Johnson, we endured our third straight losing season (6–10) in Gregg's first year. But something was different. We were headed in the right direction, ready to blossom as a contender.

Personally, I was ready for a change too, inspired in no small way by my father, Eli Williams.

BOOM BOX: THE BEST BENGALS TEAM?

It's a worthy debate.

Of the two teams in Cincinnati Bengals history that advanced to the Super Bowl—just two, and I started for both—which one was better?

I'm vouching for the first Super Bowl team.

The 1981 squad that played in Super Bowl XVI would have beaten the 1988 team that finished with a last-minute loss in Super Bowl XXIII, in large part because some of the best players from that team were in their prime years.

We had Anthony Muñoz and Max Montoya protecting Kenny Anderson, the NFL's top-rated passer, who had such consistent accuracy that if you gave him time, he could hurt any defense.

There was some great talent on our '88 team, and sure enough, Muñoz and Montoya were still protecting the quarterback. But if you pit Boomer Esiason against Kenny, I'd go with Kenny.

Muñoz was a first-team All-Pro selection at left tackle in both seasons. I've got to believe that Anthony was better in '81, his second season, than in '88. Same for Max.

Then again, maybe there wasn't much difference between those guys.

I know in my case, I was a better player in 1981—the best season of my career.

We certainly had a special defense. Three of the top sackers in Bengals history were all on that '81 unit: Eddie Edwards, myself, and Ross Browner. Our hard-hitting middle linebacker, Jim LeClair, was the only defensive player who got All-Pro honors that season. We had Ken Riley, who intercepted more passes than anybody in Cincinnati history at one corner, and Louis Breeden was at the other. Bobby Kemp was a great, physical strong safety.

The offense featured Pete Johnson, who at 252 pounds was a 1,000-yard rusher and the biggest, most powerful fullback prototype at the time. He was the Fridge before the Fridge. Cris Collinsworth was in his rookie year at receiver, but Isaac Curtis was an established star on the other side. And at tight end, we had Dan Ross. Phenomenal hands. Could catch in traffic.

Sure, the '88 team featured a prolific offense that led the NFL in scoring, with Esiason having his best season. Like Johnson, then-rookie Ickey Woods finished off many drives with touchdown plunges. He teamed with James Brooks for a nice one-two backfield punch.

Still, 1981 it is.

We also had strong-jawed leadership in head coach Forrest Gregg. We were a no-nonsense, competing team. Sam Wyche, the coach in 1988, would try to trick you if he could. Strategically, he had a creative offense. But who do you really want to play for if you're going to be a champion? Someone who is going to beat you down, face-to-face, and take the best you can offer, or someone who is going to try to trick you?

I'll take the idea of beating an opponent into submission.

Both approaches worked well enough to produce a Super Bowl berth—which the Bengals haven't sniffed since then. The path included both teams finishing with 12-4 regular-season records that allowed us to win the AFC Championship in front of our fans at home. Unfortunately, Super Bowl heartbreak was something else those teams had in common.

As well as being subjects for a healthy debate.

The earliest memory I have is my father opening the trunk of his car and pulling out equipment as he was getting ready to play baseball. I must have been three or four years old, but it left a vivid impression. My father was an extraordinary athlete himself. Born and raised in Birmingham, he was sixteen when he had a tryout with the Birmingham Black Barons of the Negro League. Another kid trying out: Willie Mays, who only went on to become one of the greatest baseball players in history. When I met Willie Mays for the first time, I asked if he knew my father. He said, "Yes, I remember your dad, but I really remember your Uncle Adolph, because he took my girl away." When he said it, you could see him go deep into his memory bank. His girl? Aunt Ethel, that's who.

That memory drove me after the '80 season. I did the math: I wouldn't be playing that much longer and wanted a son who could remember his dad playing football as his earliest memory. That was a big motivation for me.

I met Marianna Cash just before New Year's Eve in downtown Cincinnati, eating a late-night breakfast on the second-floor restaurant at the Clarion Hotel after clubbing. I don't remember who I was with, but she was with a girlfriend. We immediately hit it off. She knew nothing about football, which was fine by me. She was a budding fashion designer, a senior at the University of Cincinnati, where her father was the first black professor in the school's history. Her white mother was an opera singer.

It didn't take long for us to realize where the relationship was headed. A couple of months after we met, like in March, I was driving her home. There was something that I wanted her to do, and she said she couldn't; she needed to ask her father first. I asked her right then to make the point: If you're going to marry me, it doesn't matter what your father says. She agreed, and we were married on June 6, within three months of my proposal.

Everyone on the team was at the wedding, but none were *in* the wedding, so they could just chill and enjoy it. Forrest Gregg was there. He and his wife, Barbara, had a good time. My Dartmouth fraternity brothers were there. My line brother, Paul Robinson, brought the house down with his vocal cords while my mother-in-law, Donna, lifted the clouds as she sang.

DEMONS

We'd decided not to go on a honeymoon until after the season, but we hadn't planned on spending our wedding night at the hospital. Yet that's where we wound up after I brought my beautiful bride home to Endangered Species. Marianna had spent time with Species for the whole six months we'd been together. They were really cool with each other, which was one reason I felt we had an eternal love. But somehow, Species sensed something was different. As Marianna picked up his bowl to clean it, he bit her on the wrist. It was bad enough that I had to rush her to the hospital to get stitches. On our wedding night. Then came the tough-but-right decision: the dog had to go.

Within a week, I gave Species to a family with kids on a farm. I found the family after fielding over one hundred phone calls from potential adopters during a two-hour radio show on WLW. I culled the list of callers to a top ten, then went through the finalists. My biggest regret is that I didn't pick a Hispanic family since Species was trained in Spanish.

The 1981 season turned out to be a blast. We won the AFC Central with a 12–4 record, earning the number-one seed for the AFC playoffs and the right to host the AFC Championship Game for the first time in franchise history. Advancing to meet the San Diego Chargers in the AFC title game put us one victory away from playing in Super Bowl XVI, a dream destination with an extra layer for me since it was to be held at the Pontiac Silverdome—less than an hour's drive from Flint.

To achieve that destiny, though, we first had to survive the elements that Forrest Gregg had endured with the Packers—biting cold and a wind chill of 59 degrees below zero. What a challenge for this kid who'd grown up playing football in the snow in Flint, then had the coldest temperature I'd ever experienced during college in Hanover, New Hampshire. When game day began, no one knew how cold it was going to be. Even though we'd practiced in the cold that week, it reached its nadir on game day. It was so cold and windy. The night before the game, we stayed at a hotel in Sharonville, north of downtown Cincinnati. Usually, after finishing pregame meals and final meetings, we would drive ourselves to the stadium. This time, most of us couldn't get our cars started. So the hotel commandeered three of their shuttle vans, and we squeezed into them for the thirty-minute drive to Riverfront Stadium. Going down I-75 to the stadium was like driving through a war zone, with all the stranded cars on the side of the highway. And no one else was on the road.

Although there were thousands of no-shows—you didn't even know if your family would make it—more than 45,000 fans came and cheered like crazy. That cold was brutal. Three fans died at that game. They got drunk and took off their shirts. It was that bad. But the cold became the ultimate adversity test for a football player.

They canceled our pregame warmups for the first time while we all figured out what to wear with our uniforms. A lot of guys had on pantyhose or extra sweatshirts. While we were waiting in the locker room, I decided to go outside to see just how cold it was. All I had on my upper body was a T-shirt. I looked in the stadium bowl and it was totally empty. Freezing. You could see the cold rising, just like when it's really hot and heat rises. The cold was visible. But I knew I had to walk right back into the locker room where everybody was waiting for me. I went back and said, "Haaaah! I'm invigorated! I'm going to play bare-armed! Who's with me?" There was silence, then Anthony Muñoz said, "I'm with you." Then Max Montoya: "I'm with you." The whole offensive line went bare-armed. That was the epitome of "sun's out, guns out." Now, it's an expected part of NFL culture. No matter how cold it is, players are going to show off their biceps and their toughness.

Before that, everybody basically took their cue from the "Ice Bowl," the 1967 NFL Championship Game in Green Bay. You look at film from that game, and you can see every single player was bundled up. In our case, in 1981, San Diego's whole team was bundled up. It was so unfair for the Chargers. Their first postseason game at Miami was one of the best games of the twentieth century. That's when Kellen Winslow had to be helped off the field because of cramps. It was like eighty-plus degrees. Then they flew home to San Diego before coming to Cincinnati. The temperature change was 130 degrees for them. They talked about intimidation, especially from our offensive line. Dan Fouts, the Chargers' quarterback, could not get a good grip on the ball, but Kenny Anderson played that whole game bare-handed; he didn't put a glove on. Fouts tried to do that, but he ended up throwing quails.

I wore big, black, rubber scuba diving gloves. I had an arm pad but nothing underneath. Basically, I had no sleeves. That year, the NFL also happened to debut an experimental, heated bench. They were these hard, plastic shelves with spirals of actual fire and coils going underneath it with little holes that let the heat out. So, you'd be sitting between these holes...or *on* the holes. I remember Eddie Edwards from Miami. He was so cold. The thing about it is, as soon as you took one step into the cold, you got slapped with it. It's a whole different world. It's surreal. But you must maintain focus; you can't start tripping. You must stare down your own shivers. Because once you start shivering, you are getting into uncontrollable emotions. And you can't allow that at the line of scrimmage. Well, Eddie's pants caught on fire. And he didn't care! He didn't move. Finally, it just singed away. He had black soot on the seam of his pants, which blended in because our new uniforms had stripes.

I played well. One of my big plays—I consider it the turn-around play of the game—came at the start of the second half. We were leading 16–7 at halftime, but San Diego was in striking range. They drove to our 38-yard line when I called a zone-blitz at the line of scrimmage, wary of Chuck Muncie's tendency to cut back on his runs. Muncie was huge, tall, and so intimidating in his uniform. The lead fullback came outside of the tackle to knock me out so Chuck could cut back, but I called for a switch with Ross Browner—an "X-stunt" in play-book parlance—and he ended up blocking air. I came around Ross and hit Chuck before he knew I was there. I stuck my face mask right into his sternum. Popped the mess out of him. He fumbled, and I held on to him as he scrambled to get the football back. Ross was right there to recover the fumble, and the drive was over. That was their next-to-last scoring opportunity. Soon after, it was on to Pontiac for us.

Personally, there was a sense of destiny to finally get to the Super Bowl. It wasn't simply because the game was being staged in my home state at a stadium I used to pass while on the way to Detroit to see the Tigers play. And it wasn't because the matchup included the coincidence of playing against my former Flint Southwestern teammate Ricky Patton, giving us the distinction of being the first high school teammates to oppose each other in a Super Bowl. It's funny. In high school, Ricky starred at linebacker, and I played running back. When we got to the Super Bowl, that had flip-flopped: I was the linebacker, and Ricky was the running back for the San Francisco 49ers.

Super Bowl XVI was destiny for more personal reasons. To get married the same year I ended up in the Super Bowl...I connect that to Marianna and to my children. My two oldest sons, Julien and Jarren, were born during seasons when we made it to the Super Bowl. That's a big part of a spiritual nexus for me.

This was to be the first Super Bowl played indoors, the first played in a northern climate, and the first where the teams almost didn't make it to the stadium in time, thanks to a massive traffic jam produced by vice president George H. W. Bush's motorcade. We almost got off the buses and walked to the stadium, which we could see while stuck in traffic.

The timing was so disrupted that we didn't even have pregame warmups. But I'll never forget something else that happened before the game: The first time I got pushed that day was when I got shoved in the back by Diana Ross. She was trying to get to the middle of the field to sing the national anthem. And you know I sang along with the woman whose impact with the Supremes was so essential to the Motown music that was a heavy part of the soundtrack of my life while growing up in Flint.

Then there was the game itself. Years later, when the Bengals brought back their Super Bowl teams for a reunion, Forrest Gregg said his favorite memory from his entire time with the Bengals was the speech that I gave at Super Bowl XVI. I looked around and said, "What is he talking about?" And Isaac Curtis said, "The speech." Ken Anderson was on the other side of me. He said, "Remember the speech?"

Everybody seemed to have a memory of it except me. I had forgotten it. Because we lost the game, it became totally irrelevant. At halftime, we were down 20–0. I was totally devastated. That was another of the games when, back-to-back, we couldn't get to the game early enough to do pregame warmups, because George Bush had traffic all backed up. So, as a team, we played very poorly in the first half. We were down by two touchdowns and then, on a punt, Ray Griffin fumbled. The 49ers recovered and kicked a quick field goal. Then on the kickoff, Archie Griffin fumbled. They recovered that too, and kicked another field goal. We were all sitting in the locker room after we finished with our individual coaches, and I was raring to go. We were waiting for Forrest to give us his speech. We were waiting and waiting, and I was sure Forrest was in the front room, thinking of what he was going to say to inspire us. I couldn't help it; I just blurted out, "We can do this! We can all win! All of us. Every player needs to play like they've played all year! Anthony (Muñoz), you're going to block like you've never blocked before! Cris (Collinsworth), when they throw that ball at you, you know you're going to catch it. Isaac (Curtis), when you get that ball, take it to the end zone. And me, I'm going to do my part."

We stormed out of that locker room. And on the first drive, our offense drove down the field and scored a touchdown. That made it 20–7. On the next possession, we just stuffed their offense. Our offense got the ball in good position and took it all the way down to the 1-yard line. We were inches from making the score 20–14 in the middle of the third quarter. Screw you guys. Then the 49ers made a goal-line stand. I've given corporate talks about that halftime speech and how beneficial it was. But in that moment on the goal line, I didn't say anything. I was just so depressed. How could we not score? How could Pete (Johnson) not get into the end zone? The ball was six inches away. That's when the speech was relevant. I didn't take that leadership opportunity then. I've never forgone other opportunities since.

We lost 26–21 with the 1981 squad that was the best team I ever played with. It will always feel like that was the Lombardi

Trophy that slipped away. We were the first team to lose a Super Bowl after outgaining the winner in total yards. Ken Anderson was the first quarterback to pass for 300 yards in a Super Bowl. Our defense was special, with great movement on the D-line. We had great corners in Kenny Riley and Louis Breeden, and secondary coach Dick LeBeau incorporated zone-blitz concepts that would ultimately help define his legacy as a coach. We had so many reasons to win, but in addition to the two fumbled returns, we lost two turnovers in the red zone.

Just horrific. Suddenly, I faced another type of demon. Losing a Super Bowl is more than just missing the opportunity for a championship. It's missing out on that legacy—that unique position in the history of the game. Look at what happened to the 49ers after they won that game. They ignited a dynasty and became the princes of the NFL, while we were left with no choice but to try again.

BOOM BOX: HOW MEAN WAS "MEAN" JOE GREENE?

I found out how "Mean" Joe Greene earned his nickname on December 10, 1977, in Cincinnati.

Let's begin with the setting. It was brutally cold, with a wind-chill of seventeen degrees below zero, marking the coldest game in Bengals history (until five years later when we played the coldest AFC title game in NFL history). The day before, Chuck Noll, the Steelers' legendary coach, slipped on a sheet of ice getting off the bus at the Clarion Hotel. He broke his arm. Day of game, he was in a sling.

Our head coach, Tiger Johnson, tricked the Steelers and changed the visitors sideline to the home sideline and vice versa. This put their bench in the shade and ours in the sun, where it was at least ten degrees warmer.

It pissed off Noll. He ran up to Tiger during pregame warmups to complain. His sling and arm were flapping as I did the ritual I'd started during my freshman year at Dartmouth—running counterclockwise around the field. Tiger was all alone. Noll was followed by his defensive line coach, George Perles, who was followed by his entire defensive line, the "Steel Curtain."

Tiger was surrounded, yelled at, and momentarily flustered by their angry reaction. Perles stepped in front of Noll and declared that he was ready to fight. None of my teammates were anywhere around. Tiger was about to get jumped! That's when I became a crazy man and ran at the Steel Curtain—Mean Joe Greene, L. C. Greenwood, et al.—yelling, "Let's start the game now! We don't need no [expletive] refs! Let's go!" They all looked at me like I was nuts. But it bought time for the real refs to run over and time for Tiger to turn, walk away, and ignore their concerns because what was done was done.

We needed to win the game by seven points to keep our slim playoff hopes alive. We kicked off to start the game. On the first drive, a leaping Lemar Parrish intercepted a pass and returned it for a touchdown. On their second drive, we forced a fumble around their 30-yard line. By the time the big pileup unraveled, the Steelers defense was on the field. At the bottom of the pile was me with the ball.

As I got up, Mean Joe was right in front of me. I remembered vividly his snarl of hate during our pregame confrontation and knew he was aching to take a shot. I looked him in the eyes, smiled, and softly lofted the ball to him as I pivoted and ran toward our bench. Before I could take three steps, I felt the loudest bang on my helmet. Mean Joe had hurled that football in a fastball spiral right at the back of my head. The crowd went silent. The ball caromed straight up at least 10 yards into the air. Every ref that had a flag threw it. Fifteen yards.

What a way to start an intense game—which we won 17-10—to keep our playoff hopes alive.

I never talked to Greene about this, but years later we were both at an event featuring former NFL Man of the Year honorees at Super Bowl LII in Minneapolis. Bygones were bygones. His disposition was so different than it had been on that cold day at Riverfront Stadium. He was most concerned and caring about the condition of my knee. At a different time and place, Mean Joe Greene was the opposite of his famous nickname.

CHAPTER 7
PRINCIPLES

WE CAME HOME AS HEROES, REGARDLESS. AFTER OUR DEVAS-
tating loss on the NFL's biggest stage, the Cincinnati Bengals
were embraced with a champion's welcome when we returned
the day after Super Bowl XVI. No, the so-called "twenty-four-
hour rule"—the well-meaning but illusory standard promoted
in NFL culture for mentally putting defeats *and* victories in
the rearview mirror—doesn't apply to Super Bowls. When
you've worked your butt off, not just for a season but throughout an entire career to reach the NFL mountaintop, it tends to
stick with you for a while when you fall short of winning it all.
Maybe even for life.

Yet losing can reveal much about character. I learned
something about the people of Greater Cincinnati after that
Super Defeat. They had our backs. It was evident as we rode
on buses from the airport in northern Kentucky, headed to
Fountain Square for a rally. So many motorists stopped their
cars, got out in the cold, and applauded. That spirit was then
demonstrated by thousands more who waited for us in downtown Cincinnati. We had left the city after playing the coldest

game in NFL history in terms of wind chill, and it was still freezing that afternoon. The elements, though, didn't stop the massive throng of fans—the greatest fans in the world—from jamming Fountain Square in the bitter cold with the same fervor they undoubtedly would have had if celebrating a Super Bowl crown.

As far as we could see in every direction, there were people. It was one of the biggest crowds ever assembled in Cincinnati history, all to show us that they went through it with us. I was so moved. Sure enough, I had another speech in me. It was one of those rah-rah, "I guarantee it" speeches. I only made one clip-and-save promise: We would get back to the Super Bowl and win it the next time. And I believed that, down to every single bone in my body.

Part of the challenge in rebounding from any difficulty—including a loss in the game you've waited all your life to play in—is to turn a negative into a positive. Losing that Super Bowl strengthened my resolve to have an impact that went far beyond football. From the day that I arrived in Cincinnati, it was important to give something back to the community. Yet in the wake of losing Super Bowl XVI, that mission became much deeper.

I felt like I was playing for a bigger purpose. I committed myself to playing for every single child in Cincinnati—but not only *on* the field. The work I began as a rookie with the Cincinnati Speech and Hearing Center was merely the beginning of a platform to serve a greater good. And losing a Super Bowl was hardly the only motivator. Being discounted at various stages in my life—like I had been in the Bo Schembechler episode—also provided fuel to use all my resources and visibility to be a difference-maker in the lives of people.

Empathy. Humility. Passion. Integrity. Inspiration. Commitment. These were some of the characteristics, I believed, that needed to define me to the people of Cincinnati, more than tackles, sacks, and interceptions. It's one thing to be a leader for one of the best teams in the NFL. But it became just as important, if not more so, to be a leader in our community.

I was also motivated by a Super Snub. Despite playing a major role on a Super Bowl team, I wasn't selected for the Pro Bowl after the 1981 season. I tried to hide that it really bothered me, but it hurt so bad.

In fact, though I'm often considered the most prolific linebacker in Bengals history, I was never chosen for the Pro Bowl a single time during my entire NFL career. Was it politics? Popularity? The size of our market? The boost that some players received for playing on teams with larger national profiles? Did the Bengals PR team promote the defensive players?

You can drive yourself crazy trying to figure it out while knowing in your heart that you deserved better. But what do you do about it? Obviously, I couldn't control the Pro Bowl balloting by players, coaches, and fans, or the votes from the media for All-Pro selections.

Ultimately, I realized that no matter how well I played, no matter how much the team achieved, I couldn't control the recognition. At Dartmouth, the honors came out of the clear blue. I had a great sports information director in Jack DeGange. He believed in me, and I was recognized for it. In Cincinnati, no matter what I did on the field, there was no recognition. I decided I just wasn't going to care about it anymore. The only thing I was going to care about was what people in Cincinnati thought of me. And that came down to an essential purpose: what can I do to make this a better community?

Above: Long before making a mark as an intense linebacker, here's the evidence that I was a natural-born charmer as the cutest baby in Flint, Michigan. (Courtesy: Williams' personal collection)

Left: My parents, Julia and Eli Williams, married young in 1952 and rarely spent a day apart for the next sixty-seven years. (Courtesy: Williams' personal collection)

Sophomore year at Dartmouth, when I stepped up to the varsity squad. The Afro was more than a sign of the times. It provided extra cushion under the helmet. (Courtesy: Dartmouth Sports Information Department)

This blocked field goal against Yale proved that I had some vertical lift to go with the sideline-to-sideline tackling. (Courtesy: Dartmouth Sports Information Department)

With my brothers of Alpha Phi Alpha Fraternity, Inc.—the first black fraternity on the scene at Dartmouth. (Courtesy: Williams' personal collection)

At my rookie camp in 1976, the Dartmouth connection with Bengals owner Mike Brown was strong. Over the years, we had strong differences, too. (Courtesy: *The Cincinnati Enquirer*)

Running extra laps after a minicamp practice in 1981 with talented tackle Anthony Munoz, the only primary Bengals player (to this point) enshrined in the Pro Football Hall of Fame. (Courtesy: *The Cincinnati Enquirer*, Jeff Hinckley)

At my wedding, Dartmouth grads Lawrence Ivey (my banker) and Harry B. Wilson (my college teammate and father to current NFL star Russell Wilson) were full of spirit. (Courtesy: Williams' personal collection)

The thrill of a special victory in 1981 after we clinched the first Bengals playoff berth of my era with a win against the Browns at Cleveland Municipal Stadium. (Courtesy: *The Cincinnati Enquirer*)

Shaking down Chuck Muncie for a fumble during the "Freezer Bowl" at Riverfront Stadium that resulted in our first trip to the Super Bowl. (Courtesy: *The Cincinnati Enquirer*)

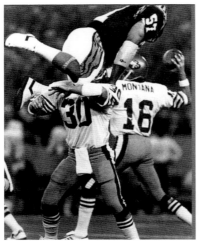

Sometimes, as in Super Bowl XVI at the Pontiac (Mich.) Silverdome, you have to take to the air to get a rush. (Courtesy: *The Cincinnati Enquirer*)

My son Julien, 2, heads back to the locker room with me after a workout in 1985. Years later, Julien would make a profound athletic mark of his own with mixed martial arts. (Courtesy: *The Cincinnati Enquirer*, Gerry Wolter)

The Cincinnati Enquirer captured the magnitude of support we received from Bengals fans at a downtown rally following our Super Bowl setback. (Courtesy: *The Cincinnati Enquirer*)

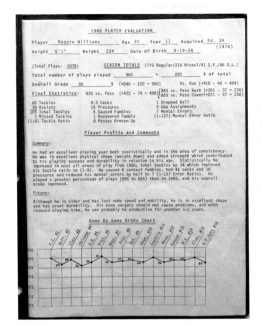

```
                    1986 PLAYER EVALUATION

Player  Reggie Williams    Age 32   Year 11   Acquired Rd. 3A
                                                       (1976)
Height  6'1"     Weight  234    Date of Birth  9-19-54

(Total Plays: 1078)     SEASON TOTALS  (775 Regular/216 Nickel/41 S.Y./46 G.L.)

Total number of plays played    960    =    89%    % of total

Overall Grade   88    % (+840 - 120 = 960)      Vs. Run (+418 - 46 = 464)
Final Statistics:  85% vs. Pass (+422 - 74 = 496){84% vs. Pass Rush (+201 - 37 = 238)
                                                 {86% vs. Pass Cover(+221 - 37 = 258)

66 Tackles           4.5 Sacks               1 Dropped Ball
39 Assists           16 Pressures            5 Gap Assignments
105 Total Tackles    6 Caused Fumbles        7 Mental Errors
3 Missed Tackles     1 Recovered Fumble      (1-137) Mental Error Ratio
(1-9) Tackle Ratio   8 Passes Broken Up

                   Player Profile and Comments

Summary:

He had an excellent playing year both statistically and in the area of consistency.
He was in excellent physical shape (weight down) and added strength which contributed
to his playing success and durability in relation to his age. Statistically he
improved in most all areas of play from 1985; total tackles by 34 which improved
his tackle ratio to (1-9). He caused 6 contact fumbles, had 4½ sacks and 16
pressures and reduced his mental errors by half to 7 (1-137 Error Ratio).  He
played a greater percentage of plays (89% to 86%) than in 1985, and his overall
grade improved.

Future:

Although he is older and has lost some speed and mobility, he is in excellent shape
and has great durability.  His knee surgery should not cause problems, and with
reduced playing time, he can probably be productive for another 1-2 years.

                   Game By Game Grade Chart
```

The annual performance review from 1986 points out that I cut mental mistakes in half from the previous year and includes a prognosis for my pending knee surgery. (Courtesy: Williams' personal collection)

Greeting President Ronald Reagan at the State Dinner in January 1988 honoring Egyptian President Hosni Mubarak, whose wife Suzanne also exchanged pleasantries. It was one of my five visits to the White House, including invitations from Nancy Reagan, Colin Powell, George and Barbara Bush, and with Sports Illustrated's Sportsmen and Sportswomen of the Year. (Courtesy: *Official White House photo*)

Although I never played in the NFL's annual all-star game, an even bigger honor came in 1987 when Commissioner Pete Rozelle presented me with the Walter Payton NFL "Man of the Year" Award during a halftime ceremony at the Pro Bowl. I was in severe pain, shortly before having microfracture knee surgery. What you don't see in the picture: The crutches that I was adamant about ditching for this special moment that acknowledged my contributions to community service. (Courtesy: Dave Boss, NFL Photos via *The Associated Press*)

Sworn in for the Cincinnati City Council in 1988 by Judge Jack Sherman, as my wife Marianna, Jarren, 4, and Julien, 5, take it in with me. (Courtesy: *The Cincinnati Enquirer*, Fred Straub)

During this visit at the home of Dr. Walter Bowers in Cincinnati in 1988, Archbishop Desmond Tutu told us that the city council action that I initiated to divest funds from the city's retirement board funds in companies doing business in or with South Africa was the "straw that broke the camel's back" in applying economic pressure on the apartheid regime as the country prepared for its first Democratic election. (Courtesy: Dr. Walter Bowers' collection)

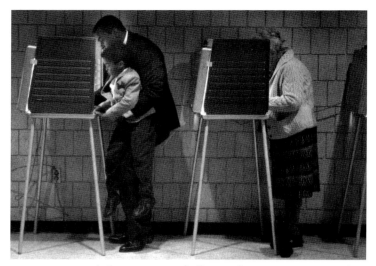

My son Jarren, 4, helps me cast my ballot on Election Day in 1988, when our vote helped me retain my seat on the Cincinnati City Council. (Courtesy: *The Cincinnati Enquirer*, Michael E. Keating)

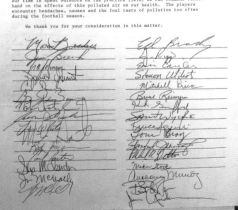

With our practice facility, Spinney Field, located in an industrial zone with poor air quality, I had no problem getting teammates, coaches, and staff members to sign a petition protesting the conditions. (Courtesy: Williams' personal collection)

Of course, Mickey Mouse welcomed me with open arms as I joined Walt Disney World. But in launching Wide World of Sports, a key was to establish a distance from Mickey and Friends. (Courtesy: Disney's Wide World of Sports)

Taking the field at Riverfront Stadium for the final home game of my fourteen-year career with the Bengals. They dubbed the occasion, "Reggie Williams Day." (Courtesy: *The Cincinnati Enquirer*, file photo)

My youngest son, Kellen, was a walk-on at Vanderbilt. He ultimately earned a scholarship and became the starting fullback. He wore No. 42 to honor Jackie Robinson. (Courtesy: Williams' personal collection)

Muhammad Ali was one of the biggest inspirations of my life. I was so honored to dine with the champ during one of his visits to Disney. (Courtesy: Williams' personal collection)

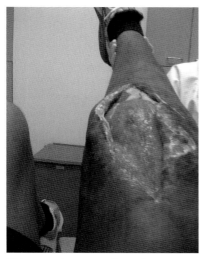

This was the state of my knee as an outpatient in May 2008, walking the streets of midtown Manhattan with a PICC line. Notice that my street shoes are on. (Courtesy: Williams' personal collection)

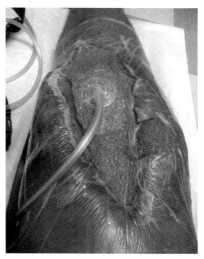

This is the suction hose of a portable pump that I carried around New York in 2008. It siphoned off the excess blood and other post-surgical fluids draining out of my knee, to ease the swelling. (Courtesy: Williams' personal collection)

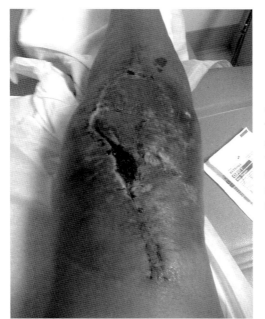

The dog days of August 2008. With the lower gastroc flap attached, ensuing procedures would shave necrotic tissue and attach a second gastroc flap. (Courtesy: Williams' personal collection)

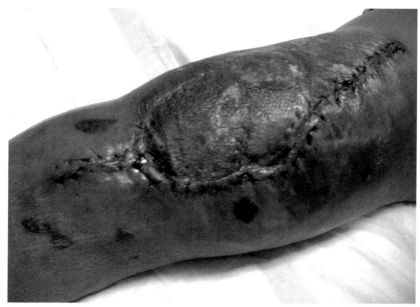

After the second gastroc flap was sewn in, in September 2008. (Courtesy: Williams' personal collection)

The aortal dissection in 2014 left me with another reminder down the middle of my chest that resilience is a way of life. (Courtesy: Williams' personal collection)

Back at Disney for the twentieth anniversary of Wide World of Sports, with old pals Goofy, Mickey, and Minnie. (Courtesy: Disney's Wide World of Sports)

Kellen keeping watch over me and my older brother, Greg—a force for me in more ways than one—going way back. (Courtesy: Williams' personal collection)

Was honored to represent the Big Green during the Dartmouth-Princeton game at Yankee Stadium in November 2019, with festivities that commemorated 150 years of college football. (Courtesy: Williams' personal collection)

In full effect at Dan Marino's charity fundraiser in Miami during the week of Super Bowl LIV in January 2020. That's a transdermal CBD patch from Pure Ratios on my knee, which helps with pain management. (Courtesy: Patrick Eckstrom)

I threw myself into volunteering and community service. I created the Reggie Williams Scholarship Fund, which provided a scholarship in every single public high school in Cincinnati. I spoke at every high school and middle school, and probably, in aggregate, every elementary school in the city. I was everywhere. I expended as much energy serving the community as I did on the football field.

This flowed naturally, building on my involvement with the hearing center. Word got around that I connected well with the kids, and the demand grew. And the things I told the kids didn't come from just reading them a book. I gave them my life experience. Remember, I'm the guy who was once too embarrassed to speak in front of my classmates in elementary school. Yet by the time I was established in the NFL, I had long since developed the gift of gab. But connecting with people goes both ways. It's not merely talking. Because I'm hearing impaired, I've learned to value listening. That too is an essential gift.

Two situations that hammered home that reality more than any other during my career amazingly spanned both ends of the players-versus-management spectrum.

Let's start with Mike Brown. In 1985, while negotiating a contract during the prime of my career, my agent received a letter from him trying to justify why they were lowballing me. He said I was the sixtieth-ranked outside linebacker in the NFL. *Say what?* I was so insulted.

Furthermore, Brown wrote this gem: "We're facing a new day, where money is tighter."

Think about that. He was pleading poverty, and the value of his franchise—which he and his father never spent a dime for—has grown to be worth $2 billion now.

I've had a unique lifetime relationship with Mike, but that letter I took very personally.

My agent, Mike Slive, talked me out of going ballistic and refocused me on why I played the game in the first place. The key was not to allow money to determine my self-worth. Besides, I never played football for the money. If I had, coming out of college I would have wound up in the CFL with Toronto, which offered me $500,000 over three years—significantly more than what I got from the Bengals.

Slive, whom we lost in 2018, is best known for his long tenure as commissioner of the Southeastern Conference. He's the one who turned the SEC into the powerhouse that it is today. His legacy includes an active role in spearheading the hiring of Sylvester Croom at Mississippi State in 2004 as the first African-American head football coach in SEC history.

When I met Slive, a Dartmouth grad, he was a judge in Hanover, New Hampshire. Before transitioning to several executive roles on the college level, he negotiated the first three of my four contracts with the Bengals. He was very diplomatic. In 1985, I wound up with a small increase and never even came close to holding out for more on that deal or any of the other contracts. It was never a business to me. It was always a love affair in search of a ring.

My last contract, I negotiated myself. I know I got hosed on it by Mike Brown. But the love I had for the city of Cincinnati, being a councilman, and giving 100 percent of that council salary to charity was the only compensation that I needed.

After my career, there were more battles with Brown over my worker's compensation claims. Just as with the contracts, the Bengals took a much harder stance than other teams around the league. And that philosophy, which for many years was reflected in the Bengals spending less on player salaries than any other NFL team—and in most instances, significantly less—is why the Bengals have never won any championships. Since the salary cap was instituted during the 1990s, they have been mandated, like all teams, to spend a minimum amount that is relatively close to the cap. Just know they're spending more than they want to spend, I guarantee you.

Still, it is startling to compare the numbers from my career to the earnings of today's players. On my rookie contract in 1976, I got a $35,000 signing bonus and a $35,000 first-year salary. The entire four-year deal was worth about $250,000—and that was after my salary doubled in my fourth year to $80,000.

Almost forty-five years later, players drafted in a similar third-round slot to mine commanded four-year contracts worth nearly $4 million, averaging more than $900,000 per year. That not only reflected inflation (my $250,000 in the 1970s would be $1.1 million in 2019), it illustrated the growth of the NFL product over the decades.

There's no part of me, though, that begrudges today's players—some of whom make more in one game than I made in fourteen years and 206 games. That's what freedom looks like with the free-agency system players ultimately gained during the 1990s.

I also know that physically, you can lose it all in one game. That's the common denominator for all players, past and present. We all get hurt. That's why totally leaving behind the pre-'93 class of former players for lifetime health benefits is what I do begrudge.

Here's another way the dollars hit home: the medical bills that I saw following my last knee operation totaled around $250,000, the entire total of my first NFL contract.

That underscores why, back in the '80s, lifetime healthcare was the key issue that moved me to cross the picket line when

NFL players went on strike in 1987. The majority of players and the leadership of the NFL Players Association (NFLPA) saw free agency as the dominant issue. I was in the minority. For me, the biggest concern was healthcare.

Looking back, crossing the picket line is the biggest regret of my life. The first issue wasn't with my teammates, it was with my dad. He was a member of the United Auto Workers union his whole life in Flint, and as a family we picketed labor situations while I was growing up, along with marching for civil rights. My father supported my decision, even though he took some flak about it at Fisher Body.

Crossing the picket line also was one of the best decisions I ever made, as it led to the opportunities that I enjoyed after football. So I have mixed feelings.

At the time, though, I was firm with my decision. When players struck in 1982, the primary demand was for 55 percent of the revenues. We shut down the game for fifty-seven days, with no picket line to cross before coming back for an abbreviated season. The collective bargaining agreement struck in '82 included severance pay and other financial incentives but no free agency and no 55 percent slice of the pie.

The 1987 strike was so different. When it was called after two games, NFL owners had an alternate plan that, technically, caused just one week's worth of games to be canceled: replacement players. Three games were staged with the so-called scabs—players who had been cut in training camp or had played in other leagues—and a handful of veterans like myself who'd crossed the picket line.

My decision, as you'd expect, fueled some serious tension with other veteran leaders on the team, most notably Boomer Esiason, the star quarterback who also was the Bengals' player rep to the NFLPA, and Cris Collinsworth. Before the strike, I hinted to Boomer that I was focused on healthcare, not free agency, but was willing to talk to him.

He invited me to his house in Kentucky after a practice, but the encounter was far different from the one-on-one chat I expected. In fact, it turned ugly. Quickly. When I arrived, I saw almost all my teammates' cars—or at least all my non-black teammates' cars—parked up and down the street. There were no defensive players there, but there were a lot of white players from the offense. Anthony Muñoz and Max Montoya were there too. The only brother in the room was Stanford Jennings, the running back, who was Boomer's friend from Furman. When I walked in, I realized this was not about listening to my point of view. It was an intimidation tactic by my teammates to influence me to not cross the picket line.

I sat on a couch and the rest of the players surrounded me. Boomer said, "You're not going to cross the picket line."

I looked around and said, "You know the first one is mine."

In other words, if they were intent on physically attacking me, I was intent on punishing the first attacker with no mercy.

I looked every player in the eyes and said, "Bunch of cowards."

I got up and walked out. It was like the dogs. It was that same moment, looking at another type of alpha male—our quarterback. The union leader. It was them against me, right there. And that's what we overcame to be in the Super Bowl the next year.

I'm very proud of the success Boomer has enjoyed, and equally so about the cystic fibrosis charity he started on behalf of his son. That's tremendous work. His children were born while we played together in Cincinnati. I know his wife, and I know his heart. But we were on different sides of the free-agency issue. He was set to become a free-agent quarterback;

I was a team player. If we were not going to have it all financially, then I believed we should have it all on healthcare.

Essentially, the goal of free agency was to make more money. When the 1987 strike was settled after three games with "replacement players," the NFLPA launched a legal battle that led to a new system in 1993 with free agency and a salary cap. But the reality of free agency is that it creates a "have and have-not" society among the players.

Even with the philosophical differences I had back then, I'd tell the players of today to always stick together. In our case, Boomer, Cris Collinsworth, and I were able to put things behind us. When the strike was resolved, I sat by myself on the bus and on the plane to minimize friction. I had my own single room, which was great. There were lingering sentiments. But we had to bury the hatchet in real time to accomplish what we did the following season: get back to the Super Bowl.

BOOM BOX: THE NIGHT L. T. TOOK A BITE OUT OF HECKLERS

Don't mess with L. T.

A couple of hecklers found that out the hard way one summer night in Chicago during the mid-1980s when they decided to taunt Lawrence Taylor...only to experience what NFL quarterbacks knew well enough about a linebacker in pursuit.

Picture this: We were seated together in a courtyard with our wives among the guests of honor at the NFL Players Association's annual awards dinner. I was there to receive the Byron "Whizzer" White Award for community service. Taylor was there for being the best player at his position. We were dressed in tuxedos for this very classy affair to benefit the Better Boys Foundation, minding our own business.

Suddenly, these two Bears fans walked by on the other side of a wrought-iron fence that was at least seven or eight feet high. They saw us and yelled: "L. T. sucks! You're full of [expletive]!"

L. T. looked at them, hopped up, ran to the fence, scaled it, ran those guys down, kicked their asses, came back like it was nothing, and didn't say a word about it. I'm thinking, "You've got to be [expletive] kidding me." I mean, he just went off!

Number one, I don't know how he got over that fence, but he did. When he was running toward the fence, the Bears fans were kind of backing away. They didn't expect him to scale it. When he was over it so quickly and was almost on them, they screamed something like, "Ahhh!" It was like a cartoon: their feet were churning, but they weren't going anywhere. L. T. caught one: *Bam!* Ran down the other: *Bam!* Then he came back to the table like it was nothing. His wife didn't say anything. No one heard about it the next day. There was no media about it.

Me? I'm thinking I didn't see what I'd just seen. Marianna kind of looked at me like, "Are you going to say something?" No. And I never talked to him about it. More than anything, it made me think: "I'm not as crazy as this dude. Maybe that's why he's the best linebacker—because I am not off like that!"

The worst scenario I ever encountered with fans went down in Houston at the Astrodome. There was something going on with construction, so we had to walk from the field up through the fans. They were all throwing food and drinks at us. All that did was serve to fire us up.

And yes, we had our helmets on.

But I've never had an individual situation get out of hand with a fan. I've had a whole lot of confrontations while on the field, with fans of other teams screaming and yelling from the stands. I'd just walk away.

In a sense, those hecklers of Taylor were asking for it. Would I encourage people to ask for assaults? Of course not. Would I assault someone who's asking for it? Probably not. And I definitely wouldn't do it in a tuxedo. But L. T. would. And did.

People often ask about the "worst" injury I suffered in the NFL. Well, there's exhibit A and exhibit B.

There was a Monday night game against Pittsburgh, probably in the early '80s, and I was flying after Franco Harris. It was a delayed draw play, and he came through the hole, wide open. I had taken a few drop-steps to my zone, then charged to defend the run. Franco did a little hop and twist. I flew right past him and into Jim LeClair, our middle linebacker. But I didn't know that. I was airborne, then all of a sudden, I was lying on the ground and one side of my body was in excruciating pain. But more worrisome, the other side of my body was completely numb. I lay on the field, hurt and paralyzed, and the only thing on my mind was, "I won't be able to hit Franco again." I was thinking he destroyed me. It was scary. The doctor ran out. I told him what was wrong, and he said, "Okay, I'm going to go and see about the other guy." What? The other guy? Maybe I hit Franco after all? If I got Franco, I had to be the first one up. The psychology was that, as soon as I knew the doctor had to see another player, my paralysis was healed and I could move. It wasn't until I got to the sideline that someone told me I'd plowed into Jimmy LeClair. Jimmy would always say that was the hardest hit of his career.

The worst pain I absorbed on the field, though, was on a goal-line stand at Houston in '87. It was Alonzo Highsmith, a rookie. We had this old veteran's adage: Don't let a rookie score standing up. If he's going to score, he's going to have to score on the ground. He was running behind Mike Munchak. To knock Highsmith down, I had to knock Munchak down. I wasn't going to get there before he got into the end zone, but he wasn't going to be standing. I flew into Munchak, who flew into Highsmith. They both went down...and I broke my face. I was on the ground and couldn't get up. I was in a fog. I saw orange on someone's leg, and I just grabbed him. I don't even know who the player was, but he helped me up and got me to the sideline. As soon as I got there, I said I was hurt. Dr. Robert Heitz Jr.—the same doctor who performed my abrasion surgery—said I looked fine. We fumbled the kickoff, and I went back for about four plays to finish the first half. Fortunately, they were all pass plays. No contact. I went into the locker room; my head was aching, but the doctor maintained that I was okay. I iced my head. Then, as we were about to start the second half, I blew my nose. And that's when I discovered that I'd broken the orbital bone, which separates your sinus from your eye orbit. My eye blew up like a balloon. I ran to the doctor and said, "Look! I told you I was hurt!" They sent me to the hospital. I saw the end of the game from the emergency room. When I got back to the stadium, Paul Brown and Sam Wyche were waiting for me. Everyone else was on the bus. And my eye was huge, black and blue.

You trust in your doctor. It's like the first time I dislocated my thumb; I trusted the trainer. The second time, I trusted myself.

Eventually, I made it to the Pro Bowl—just not as a player. After the 1986 season, I went to Hawaii to receive the NFL Man of the Year award during a halftime ceremony. The irony of the moment is stark. I was recognized with the league's highest honor for community service, which acknowledged my off-the-field mission. Yet I was barely able to stand, a reflection of my on-the-field endeavors.

A few weeks earlier, I had undergone abrasion surgery to repair my right knee, which was literally bone-on-bone after all of the cartilage had been removed in 1979. The ground-breaking procedure that Robert Heitz performed involved creating tiny fractures in the underlying bone, causing new cartilage to grow. As far as I know, it was the first successful microfracture surgery for an NFL player. It wasn't even called that back then. It served its purpose. I played three more seasons. But as I made my way to midfield to receive the trophy, I was on crutches.

I didn't want the crutches to be in the picture while I was standing next to commissioner Pete Rozelle, so I asked someone to take them away. I was standing there on one leg, and then Pete handed the trophy to me and walked away. I was on one leg, and the thing was heavier than I could imagine. It's solid. I was trying to smile, but I almost fell. Fortunately, it was one instance when I didn't have to give a speech. I didn't want to fall flat on my face either.

After all, I had too many reasons to stand tall.

BOOM BOX: DIVERSITY OF LEADERSHIP REMAINS A BIG NFL PROBLEM

It was nearly a decade into my NFL career before the Cincinnati Bengals had a member on their coaching staff who looked like me. Jim Anderson joined Sam Wyche's staff in 1984 as the running backs coach, finally breaking a disturbing pattern that dated back to high school.

Throughout my entire time at Dartmouth and during my first eight years in Cincinnati, the teams that I played for had all-white coaching staffs—a contrast to the presence of so many impact players who were African-American.

I finished my career having never had a black position coach or coordinator.

What a shame. It says something about how some people were not valued for their leadership abilities in the NFL, not to mention at the college level and society at large.

I wish I could say that only happened way back when.

Unfortunately, while more African-Americans have had opportunities since Art Shell became the first modern-era black head coach of the NFL in 1989, diversity is still a huge problem. The men in charge of roaming the sidelines represent the most visible barometer, but the problem exists too with general managers and other high-ranking front office positions in the league.

Sure, the NFL implemented the Rooney Rule in 2003, requiring teams to interview at least one minority candidate for head coach openings, then amended the policy to apply to general manager jobs. There was a wave of progress—and Super Bowl-winning success stories, including Tony Dungy, Mike Tomlin, and Ozzie New-some—but in recent years the NFL has regressed into the same old patterns that existed decades ago with regard to equal opportunity.

I know. Mike Brown stuck with Marvin Lewis as Bengals head coach for fourteen years. But that was a major exception. League-wide, just two African-Americans were hired for the fifteen head coach openings during the hiring cycles of 2018 and 2019. And when New-some stepped down in 2019, a league where more than 70 percent of the players are African-American was left with just one black GM.

The numbers tell me there's still a stigma, a long-term intrinsic belief by many in power of what leadership should look like in the NFL.

I think there are things the NFL needs to do to address this. For one, it can do a better job of helping to create a pipeline of coaches at the high school level. When I was a Disney executive, diversity was a critical prior-ity. I'm proud that we made inroads. In seeking more diverse candidates for our lifeguard positions, for exam-ple, I implored USA Swimming to bolster its pipeline. The NFL, the most powerful entity in the sport, can do something similar in football. They've got to address the unspoken stigma of leadership by black coaches, by creating a credible association for coaches as they are beginning their careers.

What about experienced coaches already in the NFL or on the college level who still don't get a shot? That's where an educational program for NFL owners is needed, so that they can understand their own biases.

PRINCIPLES

Until the effort to diversify becomes a priority, the results will lack the benefits attached to a diversified leadership, and the NFL will fail to become the socially conscious industry leader that it needs to be. Even as the league embarks on its second century, it's still a problem. And still a shame.

CHAPTER 8
CROSSOVER

MORE THAN A FEW PEOPLE THOUGHT THE BENGALS HAD A major distraction on hand as the 1988 season began: I was a full-fledged member of the Cincinnati City Council yet still manning my linebacker post in Dick LeBeau's defense. This had never happened before and hasn't since. No other active NFL player has ever been part of such a significant governing body.

It was a juggling act that tested my organizational and time-management skills, but the most crucial aspect of the dual roles was to be more than merely effective. I needed to be a serious impact player in both situations.

Sam Wyche, our head coach, initially was not in favor of this when I walked into his office with Mike Brown a few weeks before training camp to tell him what was going down. He accepted it, given the circumstances of my crossing the picket line. But he also told me, right there in front of Mike, that if my performance waned, he wouldn't hesitate to replace me. This was new territory for him too: How do you coach someone with this kind of political visibility? How do you ensure that it's not going to hurt the team? Head coaches want to be all-or-nothing leaders, but here I was released from practices every week. There was a lessening of his perceived power or control over one player and a very visible one in the locker room because of the recent strike. But the reason the opportunity existed was because I was widely known in the community. I was involved in so many things. That's why the transition was almost flawless.

Still, missing practices every Monday and Wednesday to attend council meetings (players were off on Tuesdays, when the council also met) was quite the departure from NFL routine. Wednesday, for instance, is "Installation Day," where we put together the game plan for the coming opponent. I handled it. I was so well versed in our scheme, I could have coached our defense. I didn't need as much practice time. And the less practice the better because I had so much wear and tear on my knees.

My teammates were very supportive, and some even seemed inspired. Even white players who were part of the "Boomer Showdown" gave me congrats because the uniqueness of my responsibility put everybody on notice to do their jobs...because I was doing *two* jobs. And I picked up another nickname, thanks to defensive end Skip McClendon: "Governor."

Yet certain challenges came out of nowhere. Take the weekend of our season opener. The Friday before hosting the Phoenix Cardinals, a bunch of our players got into a massive parking lot fight with some University of Cincinnati fraternity kids. We were on the Kentucky side, celebrating someone's birthday at a club. Several rookies were there, including Ickey Woods. Well, one of these college kids started hitting on one of the players' wives. Ickey was behind her and told the guy to step back. When this dude mouthed off, Ickey hauled off and knocked the crap out of him. I was like, "Oh, snap!" Management came in, separated us, and kicked everyone out of the club. They were going to let us out of the back entrance, but my teammates were resolved to go out the front door. And they wanted their resident political figure to lead the way. I came out and saw a crowd of college kids. I walked forward, and the seas parted. I looked behind me, and there was Joe Kelly with my other teammates behind him. As soon as I walked by, the seas closed, and these people attacked my teammates. The brawl was on. I couldn't throw a punch. I could respond if someone threw a punch at me, but everyone knew me. I was a city councilman. I got Marianna into the car, grabbed Joe Kelly and his wife, and got them in the car. As we were getting ready to leave, someone opened the door and sucker-punched Joe Kelly. I should've locked the doors.

The next morning, Joe was one of the guys with black eyes. But basically, the college kids got their asses whipped—no, I didn't participate in that—and it brought us closer together. And it spawned a different type of confidence. Maybe that's why we started the opening game with a goal-line stand—four plays within the 2-yard line—and we ended it with another goal-line stand. My game wasn't waning; I led the team in tackles and made the stop on fourth-and-goal that won the game. The victory set the tone for a remarkable season.

We didn't lose a single game at home. Our physical defense complemented an explosive offense that led the NFL in scoring and yards. Boomer Esiason had the best year of his career, winning MVP honors. Ickey Woods scored fifteen touchdowns and moved the needle with his "Ickey Shuffle" TD celebration. We rolled to Super Bowl XXIII, *and* I was on the city council.

What was projected to be a major distraction became inspirational for the team and the city.

How did this happen, anyway? I never harbored political aspirations, but the extensive community service work certainly familiarized me with many of the city's issues. A charity dinner following the dismal 1987 season—a swanky affair during the holidays at the Celestial Steakhouse in Mount Adams—provided a turning point. I was seated next to Arn Bortz, a fellow Ivy League grad (he went to Harvard) and an existing city councilman. The dinner conversation revolved around what I would do if I were on the council.

Bortz, heavy into real estate, liked what he heard. He contacted me a few weeks later and told me he was resigning from the council due to a potential conflict of interest related to the "Over the Rhine" development that was in the works. He asked if I'd consider accepting his seat. I agreed. Representing the Charter Party, he'd probably held that seat for three or four terms. But the council charter allowed you to appoint a successor to finish your term. In this case, I would have roughly a year and a half before running for election in November 1989. We kept it quiet for a while, but once it got out, it was huge news.

In recent years, we've seen so many athletes criticized for involving themselves in social and political issues. The most extreme case resulted in the NFL blackballing of Colin Kaepernick after he launched national anthem protests to draw attention to the killings of unarmed African-Americans and other social injustices. Another absurd case involved a Fox News host rebuking LeBron James for speaking about politics during an interview. Her throwaway punch line, "Shut up and dribble," became the title for the Showtime documentary co-executive produced by James that delved into the crossover between athletes and politics set against an NBA backdrop.

I can relate. On June 22, 1988, I became the only African-American on the nine-member Cincinnati City Council and the only active pro athlete you'd find performing this type of "crossover dribble."

I had to learn so much about so many things. The only way I was going to survive was to aggressively seek information. Putting together a personal cabinet of advisors was crucial. Key people lent their expertise: Reverend Fred Shuttlesworth, one of the icons of the civil rights movement; Nadine Allen, a long-time Hamilton County judge; Herb Brown, the highest-ranking black executive at the Western & Southern Financial Group; Dr. O'dell Owens, who later became president of Cincinnati State Technical and Community College; Buddy LaRosa, the pizza magnate who managed welterweight boxing champion Aaron Pryor; Jack Sherman Jr., the U.S. magistrate judge who swore me in.

Also, I became friends with tennis legend Arthur Ashe. Like Arthur, I was a *Sports Illustrated* Sportsman of the Year honoree. That's how I met him in New York and had the chance to ask about his advocacy in fighting apartheid in South Africa. He was the most visible international tennis star who refused to play there. And he pushed for other organizing bodies not to have any sporting events there. Almost every major city in the United States divested itself of any business holdings in South Africa in the early '80s. Now I'm on the city council facing a big piece of unfinished business: Cincinnati had tried to get the disinvestment bill passed in the early '80s, but it failed overwhelmingly.

Before that task, however, there was another unfinished quest in the football universe: winning a Super Bowl crown and in the process extracting some revenge against the San Francisco 49ers for our Super Bowl XVI setback. Never mind the criticism that came with missing a council meeting the week we were in Miami for the Super Bowl, as debate raged on cable TV franchising in the city. There was only so much juggling at that point. As I put it back then: "I'm not going to apologize for being in the Super Bowl."

After we arrived in Miami for Super Bowl XXIII, a riot broke out in that city's Overtown neighborhood early in the week. I became the liaison between the team and the Cincinnati police officers who handled our security detail. The team was never threatened in any way, but I was kept in the loop regarding the planning of additional security measures and communicated that to Mike Brown and Sam Wyche. I guess there was more juggling after all. The unrest, which began after a Hispanic policeman shot a black motorcyclist, was a reminder that despite the Super Bowl's imprint on Miami, a certain segment of the population—less affluent and in many ways disenfranchised—was consumed by so many other issues beyond a big game.

The issues in Overtown included a disconnect between the police and the community. There was a lot of resentment. After the police shooting, that boiled over. And just like the riots of the 1960s, when people were burning down their own neighborhoods, some people in Overtown started burning their community. I could see the fire and smoke, hear the sirens, right from my hotel room in nearby Biscayne Bay. On our off day, I made it my business to go to Overtown and talk to kids.

Even with the backdrop of a civil disturbance, Super Bowl week went smoothly with our practices, media sessions, and the visits from families. Then came Saturday night.

What a night that was. When we switched hotels—a traditional move for teams the night before a Super Bowl—it was the first time since the strike that I had a roommate. It was James Brooks, the running back. We all found out together at the last team meal that Stanley Wilson, our third-string running back, had disappeared. Sam came down crying, saying Stanley wouldn't be joining us. He had escaped. After he was found strung out in his room from an apparent cocaine-induced episode, our operations manager, Bill Connelly, went to get him to escort him out of the hotel. They took him down the side staircase instead of the elevator, and he took off running. He disappeared that whole weekend. Now we had this hanging over our heads. Brooks, aka "JB," couldn't sleep. Stanley was the team's best blocking back.

JB said, "My best blocker's gone. There's no way I'm going to have a good game!"

I gave him a pep talk: "You're going to have the greatest game, JB! You're going to arrive at your potential at the right time! You're going to take us to the end zone again and again!"

Then I stopped and tried to go to sleep. He kept on, "We're going to lose."

Me: "You're going to do it, JB!"

I did that most of the night. But the next morning, I felt I would have the best game ever.

Right before the game, we were on the sideline after the national anthem, and I heard a voice. The voice said: "They're coming after you on the very first play."

I looked around. *Where did that come from?* At first, I thought it was God talking to me. I heard the voice again.

"They're coming after you. You're old. You're slow. You're the weak link."

I still couldn't see anybody. Then I realized the voice belonged to a friend of mine from NFL Films who was really short. I was looking everywhere except down. He used to tell me I had some of the best highlights of any player. Now he's telling me that he'd overheard the plans for the first play over on the 49ers sideline, with the old-slow-weak rationale. Then he walked away.

My preparation for the game was already as high as it had ever been. When they introduced the defense, Joe Kelly went all crazy with excitement. I was right behind him. They announced, "Starting at right outside linebacker, councilman Reggie Williams." *Councilman?* That was the first time I had ever been introduced like that. I was so fired up, I did the Aaron Pryor pose. Then, not ten minutes later, I heard about the first play, and I was at the ultimate level of hyperactivity. I'd been insulted. And by the team that beat us in the other Super Bowl. How could you hate them more?

When they started the play, I didn't move. They were supposed to be coming at me. Where were they? They gave the ball to Roger Craig, who was running *away* from me. Then Craig gave the ball to Jerry Rice. On the first play, who would expect a reverse? They were setting me up for a one-on-one matchup in the open field with the most amazing wide receiver in NFL history. They were going right at me by sending their best Hall of Famer at me. Joe Montana was supposed to be Rice's lead blocker, but when he saw me waiting, he sort of fell down. He got back up, but then it was just me and Jerry. And as Jerry was flying around, I waited for him to get to a certain point, and then I cut off the angle to the sideline. He thought he was fast enough, and he cut it back. It was my job to contain him. I was able to hit him. My biggest regret: I made sure of the tackle rather than trying to end the guy's game right then. But if Joe Montana had tried to block me, I would have ended *his* game.

Turns out that the end of *my* game in Super Bowl XXIII became something that haunts me to this day. I never had the chance to sack Montana or deflect the game-winning pass to John Taylor or make some other big play in the final minutes of the game that would have prevented the 49ers from a last-minute comeback victory and ensured the Bengals a Super Bowl crown.

What a paradox. The best game of my NFL career was Super Bowl XXIII. I led our team with ten tackles. I had a sack on Joe and a couple of defended passes. I made some goal-line plays. I had some pressures. And the last five plays of the game were the only plays when I wasn't in on defense.

My best game was also the most devastating loss of my career.

What happened? Dick LeBeau, our defensive coordinator, decided to make a 4–1 scheme—usually a prevent defense— our base defense in crunch time. When I left the game, we had a significant advantage because the 49ers had just incurred a holding penalty to make it second-and-20. That's when LeBeau changed the defense. He took me out and put Leo Barker in as the lone linebacker. I thought he was changing it for just one play. I ran to the sideline. We gave up a first down that next play. I'm like, "You've got to be kidding!" The 49ers were now in their own territory. Then they just gobbled up yards. I'm like, "Aw, hell!" And I just stood there on the sideline behind LeBeau, trying to make noise every play, hinting for him to get me back in there. We had already lost our other defensive captain, D-tackle Tim Krumrie, to a broken leg in the first quarter. I was the veteran captain. These high-pressure, make-or-break situations were the moments when you wanted your ultimate leader to make sure every player in the huddle was focused. Barker was a good linebacker, but he was very quiet and spoke with a Panamanian accent that made it challenging to understand him. He would not have been in the huddle getting everybody focused. That's a situation where you would need someone who could get away with chastising teammates if needed. Leo didn't have the leadership ability to look at the guys in the secondary—David Fulcher, Lewis Billups, Solomon Wilcots, and Eric Thomas—and say, "It's on you guys. You got this?" John Taylor should have been covered. But the 49ers won with a 10-yard pass to Taylor with thirty-four seconds left.

I still haven't forgiven LeBeau for keeping me on the bench during that final drive. I have a lot of respect for him. There are few greater personalities in the history of football than Dick LeBeau. He's just a wonderful guy. At that point in time, he was being a coach. He was trying to launch something new against Bill Walsh that the 49ers hadn't practiced for. Too bad it backfired. I never yelled at LeBeau or vented at him; I never complained after the game. I didn't go to the media. But it was just so devastating to lose another Super Bowl to the same team…snatched away in the final seconds.

If we had won, I would've retired right then. I would've gone to the locker room and said, "My dream has been fulfilled." Instead, I decided that I couldn't let it end like that. I would come back for one more year, when the other challenge would be running for election.

I was the only city councilman willing to sign the release for NWA to perform at Riverfront Coliseum in June of 1989. They had just released their first album, *Straight Outta Compton*, which included the controversial rap song "F*** tha Police." There was a lot of sentiment to bar NWA from playing in Cincinnati, but I supported them on the principles of the

First Amendment. You can't be convicted of a crime of speech before it is spoken. I remember Ice Cube, Eazy-E, Dr. Dre, and all of them assuring me that they were not going to play "F*** tha Police" at the show. We held a press conference. Ice Cube was a spokesman. In front of the cameras the day before the concert, he said they weren't going to play any controversial songs. I later discovered, after the history of Ice Cube and these dudes was told, that part of their marketing plan was to try and launch themselves with the free publicity sparked by controversy.

On the flip side of the coin, I met with the police. They shared their contingency plans—there was three times the typical police presence for a large-crowd event because they didn't trust those brothers. Their plan was to cordon off the one gate where they were going to let everyone out, and those looking to riot would be directed down Sixth Street where the police would be waiting for them. Mounted police in full riot gear. A whole battalion.

When the concert began, I was backstage to provide oversight. They opened with "F*** tha Police." I knew what was happening. The police stopped the show mid-performance of the song and turned the lights on. People got upset and continued singing, "F*** tha Police!" in rhythm. As soon as that happened, I knew I had to get to the intersection point. I sprinted out the back of the arena, up a side street, and down Fifth Street. I cut across Fountain Square to a little passageway, and that was the intersection where the police sergeant who was leading the battalion was waiting for them. I got there, and there was the battalion in wonderful formation. They were covering the whole street, three-deep, in full riot gear. The kids were coming from the other direction, and they were all shouting, "F*** tha Police!" They were coming and were not going to stop. I ran up to the sergeant's horse, grabbed the reins and said, "You are not going to hurt these children." He said, "Well, you better tell them to get out of here or they *will* get hurt." I whirled and yelled: "Stop! You'd better turn around. That's it!" That was the benefit of a lifetime of being in front of kids. I had the scholarship fund in every single public high school. I'd sent hundreds of students to college. I was involved in Big Brothers and Big Sisters. The kids knew me and they listened. They stopped and dispersed. I was so relieved. No one got hurt. I was on the right side of history from a First Amendment perspective, supporting the song and the band. But I was also on the front lines of a potentially big snafu. If any of those kids had gotten hurt, it would have been on my watch.

Such were the issues that added to a very interesting final season in the NFL—one that nearly ended before it began. About a month before the season opener, I had arthroscopic surgery on my left knee, with the issue compounded a week later by an emergency appendectomy. I missed the whole preseason. Mike Brown and Sam Wyche came to the hospital and told me their plans. They were going to put me on injured reserve, but I didn't want to go out like that. If I had been all in on strictly politics, I would have gone on IR and campaigned full time while still officially a member of the team. That would have been the easy way. But I was a football player. I wanted to go out fighting for a championship. I told them, "Give me one shot. Let me practice the last Thursday (before the opening game on the road against Chicago). If I can practice, I should be able to play." And what goes around comes around: A starting veteran player can't lose his job due to an injury. Sam wasn't going to go for it. But Mike said he'd give me that one shot.

When I came to practice that day, I had lost about twenty pounds. Everyone on the team came for the defensive drill. Mike Brown came down, and Sam was there. They tested me by having Max Montoya, the far guard, pull and try to block me out. My job was to run our X-stunt and take the inside hit from one of our best offensive linemen. The first time, Max didn't go for the kill. But I had to know if I could take an all-out hit, so when Max got there, I popped him. Max said, "Let's do this again." Now he was ready. We met and stood each other up. "Yeah, I can go."

There was another type of punishing experience a few weeks later that threatened to determine whether I would have a second term on the city council. A few weeks before the November election, I proposed the resolution for the city retirement pension board to sell off investments in all companies doing business in or with South Africa. It was the same type of measure that Arthur Ashe had championed in Richmond, Virginia, and that had been passed by other governing bodies to disassociate with the apartheid regime...but it had failed twice before in Cincinnati.

It probably started out 8–1 against the measure, but eventually it got to the point where I only needed two people to swing. And I wound up getting those two votes in my worst moment—the only time I've ever had to apologize to Cincinnati. It was discovered that, while I pushed for the city to divest, I was personally guilty of what I was advocating against. I didn't know what stocks I had, but filings of financial data with the state ethics commission showed that I owned seventy-five shares of stock from Royal Dutch Petroleum, the parent company of Shell Oil. They did business with South Africa. It was on the front page of the *Cincinnati Enquirer*. Busted! By noon, I had called a press conference. I did a *mea culpa*, and I apologized for the embarrassing issue. Even though I didn't realize I owned that specific stock, it was true. I immediately told my financial counselor to sell the stock, but I also made a plea for two other council members to join me in doing the right thing. I got two more votes by really being a stand-up guy in one of my worst moments. The bill passed, but there was no celebration. While I got so much sympathy from established politicians for being sincere, I'm pretty sure most of Cincinnati thought I had no business messing with other countries.

A week or two later, Archbishop Desmond Tutu called my office and asked if he could meet me. *Of course!* He said he had something to tell me.

Tutu came to Cincinnati within weeks. We had a private meeting at the home of Dr. Walter Bowers. He told us that the legislation we had passed was the straw that broke the camel's back in South Africa. He also told us that Nelson Mandela would be released from prison in a matter of weeks and that they were planning for their first Democratic election in 1996. I'm sitting there thinking: *Wow! I lost two Super Bowls, but this is way bigger than that.*

Election Day came without a hitch. I needed to place among the top nine finishers in at-large balloting to keep my seat. I finished in the top half, with more votes than several candidates with much more political experience. I'm sure that some of my Bengals teammates voted for me...and some of them probably didn't. Regardless, I had the official swearing-in ceremony in the locker room—an ultimate symbol of the crossover between my sport and my politics.

I was hardly finished on the football front. My final weeks as a Bengal included the personal honor of a Reggie Williams Day celebration during my final home game. There was a great compliment too from LeBeau, who asked me if I was sure I wanted to retire after I collected two sacks in my final game. That was an acknowledgment that I still had something left to offer.

I finished my NFL career with a need to give something back to the Bengals players—those who were with me during my swan song and those of the future. Our team headquarters, Spinney Field, was not an environmentally safe workplace. It sat in the middle of a toxic wasteland near several chemical plants. I got signatures from just about everybody on the team—from Sam Wyche and at least forty-five players, including Boomer Esiason—protesting the conditions at the city-owned facility and proposing to the council that it be condemned. I went around the locker room and got it signed— quite the contrast to the tension during the players' strike.

There was no dissension on this issue. One day we were in practice, and there was a big explosion at one of the nearby plants. You knew it was something bad when you felt the fireball. You knew someone had died. And someone had.

Fortunately, the Bengals moved from Spinney Field. Unfortunately, it took ten years. The team ultimately moved to Paul Brown Stadium when it opened in 2000. After the Spinney facility was taken over by Hamilton County, the soil was decontaminated as part of a massive industrial cleanup. The facility is now used as a police training academy.

That's what progress looked like in Cincinnati versus progress at Walt Disney World, where we launched a business in less than half the time. It's the difference between the public sector and the private sector.

It was also as good a sign as any that it was time for me to move on to new challenges.

BOOM BOX: THEN AND NOW, THERE'S NO NEED IN OUR SOCIETY FOR WEAPONS OF MASS DESTRUCTION

If I had somehow issued a warning of the potential of all the senseless tragedies that have occurred in America in recent years with mass shootings—in schools, churches, malls, and other venues with large gatherings of people— they would have accused me of being hysterical.

In 1989 as a member of the city council, I proposed an ordinance that would have banned semiautomatic weapons in Cincinnati.

Then, like so many cases now, the measure failed for political reasons.

This is so sad.

I still can't understand why, at close range, you need that kind of firepower. It's easier to try to hide a semiautomatic handgun on your person than it is to conceal an AK-47 or some other military-style weapon.

Yet the politics worked against my proposal and my common sense.

For as much time as I spent in schools, protecting kids was my priority. I've always wanted our schools to be the safest places possible as opposed to places with so much vulnerability. I just can't imagine kids being scared of being shot up in school.

That was my most unimaginable nightmare as I tried to pass the legislation back in 1989. It's still a nightmare.

It's only gotten worse in the years since. Back then, shooters weren't killing kids in schools. They weren't going into churches. You just can't understand the immorality of people who commit such atrocities, in many cases with legal access to guns. You'd like to believe that you can spot these crazy people, but too often you can't.

And now, every time we have these mass shootings, no one does anything.

What it says to me is that I didn't fight hard enough while in political office because America is going backward with these outrageous gun laws and policies influenced by the National Rifle Association.

With all due respect to the right to bear arms, why does anybody need a gun?

I've never owned a gun. I've shot a gun. I've taken concealed-carry classes in the past because I thought I needed one when I was living in Punta Gorda, Florida. But I've always believed in managed confrontations. If we can't get along, we should be able to talk about it, and if we can't talk about it, let's just not kill each other.

Plus, I don't trust myself with a gun. There are too many accidents that can happen just by virtue of having one in your house. People can become incredibly angry, and having a gun in those situations can be a bad combination.

An even worse combination, though, are laws allowing semiautomatic weapons in what we like to think is a civilized society.

CHAPTER 9

TRANSITIONS

IN MY DREAMS, I WAS THE ULTIMATE WINNER. SUPER BOWL XXIII. Miami. Instead of being on the bench at the end of the game, I was on the field making the plays that would beat the San Francisco 49ers. These images kept coming back after I retired from the NFL in 1990. Vivid dreams of the same Super Bowl. The coach did the right thing at the right moment, and I was the difference that allowed the Cincinnati Bengals to hoist the Lombardi Trophy as NFL champions. I saw myself celebrating. The confetti felt so real. I was exhilarated. Nothing in life had ever felt that good. We won!

Then I wake up and realize it didn't happen. It's a nightmare. The euphoria is fake. It's depressing. And the nightmare is what's real.

You hear about players having different issues, mentally, when their careers are over. Well, I had some of those same things going on. I don't have those dreams now. I got to the point where I was so busy with other things that I didn't have time to have bad dreams about that Super Bowl. But for a while, it haunted me. The dreams were part of my transition.

If we had won a Super Bowl, I never would have even thought about leaving Cincinnati when I gave up my city council seat for a role as an executive in the NFL's start-up international league. Becoming general manager of the New York/New Jersey Knights of the World League of American Football (WLAF) was certainly suited to my interests, background, and potential as an industry leader. But the dilemma wasn't just about that. It also hinged on whether to leave behind the opportunity for a higher political office.

I contemplated running for Ohio lieutenant governor on a ticket with Joel Hyatt. As founder of Hyatt Legal Services, Joel later became a household name known for his punch line on national commercials for his firm: "And you have my word on it!"

Hyatt, the son-in-law of Senator Howard Metzenbaum, was planning to run for governor in 1992. He was also a Dartmouth guy. He approached me to try to bring the southern part of the state to Columbus. He had a big following in Cleveland; I had a big following in Cincinnati. We tested running, and tested very well. I also had the support of Senator John Glenn. I'm pretty sure we would have won. Yet there was a certain part of politics that didn't appeal to me anymore. That was the decision. I had already decided that local politics, like trying to become mayor of Cincinnati, wasn't something I was going to continue to pursue. It was so divisive where I was living. I was an independent; it was a conservative area. I made enemies with Republicans, and the Democrats were aloof. There's a certain maverick security in being independent and the only African-American on the city council. But I didn't want to stay in that arena.

It was a difficult decision, influenced so much by losing those Super Bowls. It stung that I didn't deliver the championship I had promised. But when I left for the WLAF, my expectation was to one day return to Cincinnati as general manager of the Bengals. Although I never talked to Mike Brown about that specifically, I felt the Knights job would effectively groom me for that position. Besides, it was Mike who'd initially approached me about the Knights job, with a wink and encouragement from his father. Mike helped put me on that track. And if it led to a return to Cincinnati, there was a certain symmetrical appeal. I couldn't deliver on the Super Bowl promise as a player, but I could provide that championship as a GM. I could do it like Ozzie Newsome, who never won a Super Bowl as a player but became a well-respected GM—the first African-American GM in NFL history—and built the Baltimore Ravens teams that won two Super Bowls. I have a lot of respect for Ozzie for accomplishing that. What a remarkable career. He was an All-Pro tight end who, along with Kellen Winslow, helped change the position, then went on to become All-Pro as a team executive.

In all the years since I left the city, Mike has had that GM role, and the Bengals have not won a single playoff game. Not one. In my mind, if I had become GM, the only way I'd still have that job would be because we had won championships. Mike doesn't hold himself or his executive daughter, Katie Blackburn, accountable to those same standards. But I would have been held to those championship standards. It's one of those spiritual contributors to why the Bengals have fallen into a lifetime of malaise. It's a curse. Just like the damned Super Bowl losses.

As it turned out, I had a two-year stint with the Knights until the NFL abruptly pulled the plug on the spring league venture. Coached by Mouse Davis, father of the pass-happy run-and-shoot offense, we were 11–10, including a playoff loss, over the two seasons when we played our home games at Giants Stadium. Hey, we won a division title in our inaugural season. But we had a terrible time trying to get the best of our cross-Atlantic Ocean rival, the London Monarchs, beating them just once in five tries—which helped boost the league's popularity in England because they were beating the Americans, and New Yorkers at that.

Our most accomplished player? That came later. I'm proud to say our backup quarterback in 1992, Doug Pederson, coached the Philadelphia Eagles to their first Super Bowl triumph.

I probably wasn't the best GM in the WLAF because at that time I was still too competitive. I hated losing. When we lost, it affected me more than it should have for a non-player in the front office. But overall, it was such a rich experience, and that started at the top.

The Knights were owned by Robert F. X. Sillerman, who built an entertainment empire, SFX Entertainment, that grew out of his expansive collection of broadcasting properties. A DJ at one of his stations was Howard Stern, which says something about the footprint he had in the industry. In the years since, Sillerman acquired rights to a majority share of Elvis Presley's estate, Graceland, in addition to the iconic TV series *American Idol,* and to, ironically, Muhammad Ali Enterprises.

With the Knights, one of the local franchise responsibilities that the league passed on was the cost of housing and feeding the players. Because of the shorter season and the fact that they weren't paying the players enough to afford housing, we had to have hotel and catering deals, so Bob was hustling. He was used to hustling, which is what you do in the radio industry. He would barter radio time to get hotel space. Well, one time the whole team got kicked out of a hotel because one of his barter deals fell through and the station wasn't going to run the ads that were traded. All of a sudden, we made a deal with another hotel of lower quality, and I had to get everyone moved immediately. There were all kinds of crazy things like that.

It's weird that I had no idea I would be working for Sillerman when I left Cincinnati. I thought that it would be an NFL-owned and -managed franchise and that I'd be working with Giants GM George Young and communicating with team owner Wellington Mara. And sure enough, my office as Knights GM was at NFL headquarters. It wasn't until after I arrived in New York, though, that I met Sillerman, who had bought into the league.

We met at his office in Midtown Manhattan. I was immediately struck by his impressive taste in art. He was very smooth, and he gave no indication at the beginning that he was going to be anything but the most compliant owner, that he was really thrilled about this opportunity and had heard nothing but great things about me, blah-blah-blah.

Ultimately, I'm thinking the NFL and other owners said, "This guy is a loudmouth headache. Let's kill the whole league. Is that the only way to get rid of this guy?" He eventually sued the league like Donald Trump did years earlier with the United States Football League.

Sillerman was so eccentric. He loved to play basketball, which is why he invited me and a few other people for a game on the indoor court at his mansion on Long Island. Well, the ceiling of his court was the glass bottom of a swimming pool. And while we played, he had naked girls swimming in the pool above us. When you were looking to take a shot, it was a distraction! He always had the home-court advantage because he wasn't looking. But it was stunning. To spend that kind of money on something like that is genius and definitely a show-stopper. But that's the kind of guy he was.

He was also the type of guy who left it to me to tell the staff that the league had folded and that everyone was suddenly out of a job. It was a total surprise. Sillerman didn't even give me a heads-up. I didn't see it coming at all when they had the conference call to tell the GMs that they were disbanding the league.

As fast as I found out about the fate of the Knights, though, another opportunity knocked. Literally. I had just signed all the paperwork to terminate my employment with the WLAF. I had no idea what I was going to do next. I hadn't talked to anyone. While sitting there in someone's office at NFL headquarters, Jim Steeg walked in and introduced himself. Steeg headed the NFL's Special Events Department and, as much as anyone, was responsible for growing the Super Bowl into the weeklong festival that it has become.

With Super Bowl XXVII a few months away in Pasadena, California, the NFL had a problem. The issue stemmed from the Rodney King riots that brought Los Angeles to its knees in April of 1992. The NFL really needed someone to spearhead a community initiative that could take the pressure off the league and the Super Bowl.

Of course, the Super Bowl had the reputation of being this huge party, where all these major business people, celebrities, dignitaries, and other bigwigs would fly in on their private jets, take over public facilities, inconvenience the community, and then leave. But this also reflected one of the lessons learned by the NFL for the indifference it demonstrated (and much-deserved criticism it received because of it) after the riots broke out in the Overtown section of Miami during the week of Super Bowl XXIII.

Steeg was inspired to leave a legacy behind in LA that would show some social responsibility and limit some of the backlash the NFL absorbed for having its grand event cast as something for the haves in an area of have-nots. Because of my city council experience, the NWA situation, and because I was a point person for the Bengals during the riot in Overtown, he said I was perfectly situated to be credible. He said, "People are going to give you the benefit of the doubt until you come up with something." I had three months to devise a concrete plan. The pressure was on me to take the pressure off the NFL for being an insensitive corporate partner.

Why do it? First off, it was a unique challenge. I would have the independence of reporting directly to Steeg up until we announced the NFL's community project on the Tuesday of Super Bowl week. But if you know me, you know I'm always trying to make a difference. It was a case where opportunity met responsibility—for me personally as well as for the league.

I started with the notion that whatever I came up with would provide a long-term benefit for kids, with a focus on improving educational resources. I was a complete outsider, but I was no stranger to the types of issues that existed in the urban areas of Los Angeles, many of which were similar to challenges that Cincinnati and my hometown, Flint, Michigan, faced. I spent a lot of time down in Compton and went to work with people in the local community, listening to those who had opinions about what could be done but were not being heard. I wound up at the Watts-Willowbrook Boys & Girls Club, which was the one facility trying to serve the needs of the kids of Compton. It was an aha moment. It embarrassed me to see how poorly maintained the facility was. The basketball floor, a patchwork of different repairs, had ripples in it. The small, cramped facility didn't have showers. It didn't have rooms for special events or tutoring or anything like that. It was worse than any Boys & Girls Club or YMCA that I had ever seen. I knew that if I did nothing more than develop a respectable place for kids, we would accomplish something that was sorely needed.

That was the inspiration for what became the NFL's first Youth Education Town (YET)—a concept that was repeated for several years in other cities that hosted Super Bowls. The 20,000-square-foot educational and recreation center went up in the Gateway Plaza—a strip mall on the same corner of Rosecrans and Central avenues where the riots started after the Rodney King verdict came down. It's the same place where a Taco Bell restaurant was burned to the ground, then rebuilt in forty-eight hours. The people of the community wanted the center. They needed a place to call their own. They needed a safe place for their kids. They needed a place where kids would be exposed to the latest technology. They needed a place that could be a resource for basic needs, as there were some kids who went to school without a hot shower. They needed a place where tutors and organizations could create programs that would positively contribute to everyone who lived in the community.

I was consumed with helping these kids and negotiated sponsorships with several companies, including Sony and Digital Equipment Corporation. *Sports Illustrated* sponsored the library at the heart of the educational resource efforts. And there was a huge assist from Garth Brooks, the country music star who sang the national anthem at Super Bowl XXVII. He held a benefit concert and donated $720,000 to the cause. The center was completed within ninety days after the Super Bowl, with funding to operate it for the first five years.

It was the least the NFL could do to give something back to a South Central Los Angeles community that by 1993 had sent more than one hundred players to the league. Why not?

For it to be successful in this particular environment, though, YET also needed the support of a specific constituency: LA gangs. For years, the turf battles between the notorious Bloods and Crips terrorized and divided the community. There was so much senseless violence related to the gangs. That's why building a safe place included insulating the walls to make sure the facility was bulletproof. If there were drive-by shootings, the kids would be safe inside. Beyond that, we needed an agreement between these rival factions that the YET would be off-limits, a neutral zone that was not going to be "tagged" as affiliated with either of the gangs. In South Central, the mentality was such that those who supported the Crips would not want to go to a place controlled by the Bloods and vice versa. At that time, there were streets you could not go down if you were wearing the wrong color. Blue was for Crips, red for Bloods. The potential for violence was devastating. I learned this and was like, "Really?" I changed clothes sometimes if I knew I was going into someone's territory. I'd wear any color *but* blue or red.

It was against this backdrop that the legendary Jim Brown made a tremendous impact. Brown might have been the greatest player in NFL history and a Hollywood star, but there was also no one more significant when it came to efforts to broker peace between the Bloods and the Crips. Through his Amer-I-Can Program, Brown was active in gang mediation as well as a mission to help former convicts develop skills that would allow them to build productive lives after being incarcerated. Over the years, he even held summit meetings between rival gang members at his home in the Hollywood Hills that resulted in no violence—which in itself symbolized the respect Brown commanded.

I met with Brown and told him about the whole project and my goal. He had a lot of personal credibility with both gangs and was able to call a meeting for them to hear my spiel. Jim wasn't going to give my presentation. He didn't say anything, really, in what was the most intense meeting of my life.

To this day, I don't know where the meeting was held. It was somewhere in South Central. Some gangbangers picked me up at my hotel with Jim in the backseat. They put me in the backseat and blindfolded both of us. Then we started driving. The whole time in the car, I was quiet, realizing what I had gotten myself into. We made all kinds of turns. The guy parked the car and told me, "I'll come and get your door." While we were sitting there, Jim leaned over and said, "Whatever you do, when they take the blindfolds off, don't look at their eyes." I'm like, "What the hell does that mean?" Like that's your *last* piece of advice? *Don't look at their eyes?* So, of course, that's the first thing I wanted to do. Why was he telling me not to look at their eyes?

It was nighttime. We were led into a nondescript house through a side door. It was similar to the layout of the house in Flint that I grew up in. You could go downstairs or upstairs into the kitchen. As soon as we walked in, they directed us downstairs, with the blindfolds still on. It wasn't until I got downstairs and we were in front of the gangs that they took my blindfold off. It was kind of dark in there. And the basement was packed. There must've been forty people there, probably twenty Bloods and twenty Crips. Everyone was strapped. As soon as we got down there, Jim didn't do any preamble. He said, "I want you guys to hear what Reggie has to say." That's all. He didn't give a supporting statement or anything! It was my spiel, and they were all looking at me. That's when I looked into the eyes of a couple guys, and the thing that I saw immediately was all the black teardrop tattoos. Those symbolized the people they had "offed"—that they had killed. Some had murdered more people than I could quickly count, and others had done even more. Then I knew what Jim had meant. I was looking at murderers. It was kind of hard to speak without stuttering. I lowered my eyes and spent the rest of meeting looking at their torsos and weapons. That's how I knew they were all armed.

I told them that the YET wasn't being built for them. It was being built for their sons and daughters. For their brothers and sisters. For every single child in the neighborhood. I told them what we were going to build. That it would be a safe place where every kid could get a great education and get the support of the community to make sure they'd have career opportunities beyond what they were doing in a gangbanging existence. I made it very personal, saying that it was about their families. I gave them the full pitch; I didn't try to sell them. I was matter-of-fact, but the bottom line was that whether a Blood or a Crip, they all had the same love for their kids and their little brothers and sisters. I explained that this was an opportunity for every-one in the room to ensure that the next generation would have the maximum amount of opportunities.

Someone on the right, someone on the left, they both nod-ded. Then they blindfolded me again, had a discussion by themselves, and informed Jim that they had agreed to not tag the place.

A name that shouldn't be lost with this effort is Wesley Buford. May he rest in peace. He was the community activist aligned with the owners of the shopping center who presented this opportunity at a great price. At the time, the shopping mall had zero value; they couldn't get any tenants. But if he could get me to go in there, I could get the space for virtually nothing. Wesley was also the person who took me to the Boys & Girls

Club. He was 75 percent great community activist and 25 percent gangster.

He's also the one who knew enough about the climate in the neighborhood to insist that we needed to negotiate an agreement with the rival gangs. That led me to getting Steeg to introduce me to Jim Brown.

Later, we learned the truce they'd accepted for the YET extended into the neighborhood and continued for at least two or three years...until someone got shot and there was war again.

After we announced our plans for the center early during Super Bowl week—complete with Garth Brooks standing behind a podium in Compton—the reviews were so positive. I approached the National Association of Black Journalists, and a bunch of the brothers and sisters showed up at the press conference. They wrote glowing stories about the NFL finally doing the right thing. And so many others in the media turned out, expressing similar sentiments. It's interesting that the NFL's commissioner, Paul Tagliabue, didn't even come to the press conference. But I didn't need his permission. I already had it funded by Garth Brooks and other sponsors. Tagliabue flew past on the way to his own press event. Yet after the reviews came in, he became much more positive about it.

Fortunately, the YET wasn't the last facility I would conceive and build.

BOOM BOX: IF I WERE NFL COMMISSIONER...

Ever wonder what a Reggie Williams administration would look like if I ran the NFL?

I have.

I'm honored to have been invited to apply and interview for the job of NFL commissioner in 2006. Obviously, I didn't win the position to succeed Paul Tagliabue. Roger Goodell was seemingly groomed for the job while working his way through the ranks at NFL headquarters and rising to the level of a Tagliabue lieutenant. Yet with my wide-ranging experiences, I think in another sense I was groomed for the role too.

Plus, every time I hear Goodell getting booed at the NFL Draft, it adds to my belief that I could have done a better job.

Number one, as the first African-American commissioner of any of the major pro sports leagues, you'd have a diverse array of coaches, general managers, and front office personnel. The pipeline would be fluid from bottom to top in every aspect of the NFL. I can speak to that with confidence because that's the kind of organization I built with Walt Disney. We were always looking for the best talent, and we looked everywhere rather than just in our old boys' club.

You always hear that each of the thirty-two teams makes its own call when hiring, which is true in the technical sense. Yet as commissioner, you can mandate. And you can create incentives, using draft capital in the equation, that would encourage owners to put more emphasis on diversifying their staffs. Also, the Rooney Rule requiring teams to interview at least one minority candidate for head coach openings would have more teeth. I would not be afraid to severely punish teams that conducted sham interviews and didn't adhere to the spirit of the rule.

Bottom line, diversity would be valued. There's no reason why Roger Goodell can't have a league-wide, team-mandatory diversity program that extends to all their hiring at every level and position. It would ensure a pool of candidates that reflects the fans that are paying money to go to the games and supporting the sponsorship of the games. Diversity is just good common sense. Good business sense.

Speaking of business principles, there would be more opportunities for minority-owned companies to work with the NFL. So you'd see the diversity on that front too.

Also, when it comes to expanding the league internationally, I would have focused on putting franchises in Canada and Mexico before pursuing London. I know there's no NFL franchise in London, per se, but the increasing commitment to play games in England and constant talk about existing franchises (like the Jaguars and Chargers) moving there illustrates how the league is developing the market. It was the long-term vision way back in the early 1990s when I was a GM in the World League of American Football.

I think it's gotten to the point where London would support an NFL franchise. But I would have put franchises in our country's closest neighbors first.

Of course, marijuana wouldn't be a banned substance in the NFL's drug policy, if I ran the league. It's a much safer, less harmful way of dealing with the pain from this physical sport than the opioids that have inflicted such damage on players and ex-players in multiple ways. The NFL needs to be on the right side of history here, on the right side of the research. They are being negligent in not allowing for the possibility of natural medicine to significantly improve some of their worst medical emergencies, such as concussions. You won't know until you study it.

It should come as no surprise, either, to know that I'd do more to support retired players—especially those in the pre-'93 class whose pension and benefits pale by comparison to the players who came after the game-changing labor deal that resulted in liberalized free agency. Lifetime healthcare would be a start in addressing their issues. I'd leave no former player behind.

The NFL under my leadership would take a strong position on a lot of societal issues too, including gun control. They're content with taking advantage of their success as the number-one sport in America and the number-one TV viewing event, but they don't use their platform well enough to help society. And there's no way we would have stopped building Youth Education Towns in every city that hosts a Super Bowl. I'm not saying that just because I established the NFL YET concept. I'm saying it because it makes a difference in underserved communities.

Yeah, "Reggie Williams, NFL commissioner," has a nice ring to it.

But believe me, as a man with political experience on my resume, it would have never been a case of empty campaign promises.

"What would you do?" Michael Eisner's question was so familiar. It was the same thing Arn Bortz had asked back in Cincinnati when picking my brain about city council matters. It was the same thing Jim Steeg had asked after telling me about his Super Bowl problem. It was the same thing I'd heard from Hank Bullough, one of my former coordinators with the Bengals, near the end of a close game. I'd made a game-clinching

sack. If he had asked me twenty more times, I would've had twenty more sacks.

Yet in the spring of 1993, it was Eisner, chairman and CEO of The Walt Disney Company, feeling me out as I had lunch with a former Dartmouth classmate, Mike Montgomery, in the executive dining room at Disney's corporate headquarters in Burbank, California. Montgomery had become so successful after graduating and was, by this point, Disney's treasurer. Eisner had a Dartmouth connection too: two of his sons went to Dartmouth and played on the varsity hockey team.

He came to the table and said that, in addition to the NHL expansion franchise that Disney founded—the Mighty Ducks of Anaheim—they were thinking about starting a sports business on an expansive swath of land adjacent to Walt Disney World in Florida.

What would I do? I had never met Eisner until that moment, but it seemed destined to happen. I gave him instant feedback. "Number one," I told him, "I'd want this place to be a communal competition site." In Flint, we had Atwood Stadium— the central stadium in the middle of Flint where all four high school teams played. It was the second stadium in the country to get Astroturf. That's where I scored my first and only offensive touchdown as a fullback. But it was something special. I told him I would expand that concept to Walt Disney World so everyone from the four corners of the country could all meet to compete. I also told him they should have a marathon to show how diverse their theme parks are. You could run the whole marathon on their property. I gave him a whole bunch of other suggestions too.

He found that interesting and asked that I follow up with a couple of people. He sent me to interview with Jack Lindquist, who was the president of Disneyland. It was my first time there. I wasn't a Disney fan, really, because Disney did not market itself to the African-American community at all. I had never been to Disneyland or Disney World. I was so impressed with the cleanliness. My kids went and enjoyed the park while I interviewed. Then I was flown to Orlando, and I interviewed with Tom Elrod and Al Weiss. One position was for an operating job. I'd build a business and run it. This would have been under Weiss, who at that time was the vice president of resorts. He wanted to hire me to create this paradigm around incrementalism by bringing in a bunch of kids Disney was unable to attract because they spent their summers going to sports camps and competitions, rather than vacationing at Disneyland. It was incrementality that really brought value to the business. The other job was in marketing, using sports to tell the story of Mickey Mouse and the theme park, which in a way they were already doing. They'd march characters out to the competitions or use other forms of promotions to try to create pixie dust to connect with young athletes. That was not the best way for me to launch a business with Disney if I wanted it to survive long term. It had to be authentic.

That's why it almost didn't happen. I had a philosophical disagreement with Elrod, who had previously worked for the Amateur Athletic Union (AAU). He believed that you had to incorporate the Disney characters into the competitive backdrop, and if I was going to work for him and join the team, I would do it his way. Well, at that point in time, I was not going to accept a job at Walt Disney. I had two more interviews that day. My next interview was with Linda Warren, of all people. I went into her office and I was totally chill. I put my feet up and said, "I'm not coming here for a job." Elrod was her boss. I told her, "This guy is a bully, and I'm not going to work for him. And I doubt that I can work for Al Weiss either, if he has more stripes. I'm not coming to

Disney." That's when Judson Green—who was both Weiss's and Elrod's boss at the time—called and told me he would protect me from Tom Elrod. I decided I'd work for Al. They gave Al a promotion. He got even more stripes. He became a senior VP, just under being an executive vice president. Judson was a supporter of my vision. Interestingly, he's a concert pianist too. It was our mutual love of music that helped us develop a unique relationship. He stepped up.

I took the job, but I did so with a chip on my shoulder. It was only the beginning of the hurdles I faced—in more ways than one. When I showed up at Walt Disney World for my first day as director of sports development, I was just the second African-American executive on-site, joining Bob Billingsley in that distinction. But a funny thing happened right off the bat that illustrated just how rare an achievement that was.

The ID badges for executives at Disney contain a gold stripe. Yet the white girl managing the HR desk refused to give me an ID with a gold stripe because, well, it seemed apparent to me that she couldn't believe—or accept—that a black person was an executive there. I had to go to my car, pull out my paperwork, and get her supervisor. Only then was the issue fixed. Then I began the orientation program for new employees and saw the Disney historical film *Disney Traditions*. It included images of Al Jolson—the poster boy for blackface—singing "Mammy." I was incensed. That's where my protest began—on my second day on the job. This wasn't a dream. It was a reality that further defined my purpose.

CHAPTER 10

AUTHENTICITY

WHEN DISNEY'S WIDE WORLD OF SPORTS COMPLEX OPENED in 1997, the expansive, state-of-the-art complex near the theme parks was off-limits to Mickey.

Yeah, *that* Mickey. The Mouse. Goofy and Minnie, because they were friends of Mickey, couldn't come either. Goofy especially. He was like the one bad uncle who killed the whole family. There was no way I'd have a Goofy character at an authentic sporting event.

That may seem sacrilegious. Disney was built on those mouse ears. Millions of children came from across the globe to bask in the pixie dust of Walt Disney World in Florida and Disneyland in Southern California—signature anchors for one of the biggest players in corporate America.

Yet to build a sports brand at Disney and to establish credibility as a serious athletic venue that could consistently attract legitimate competition—and the kids that came along with it—I believed we needed to separate our business from the tried-and-true staples reflected by Mickey Mouse and friends.

As you might suspect, this philosophy earned me some significant corporate enemies after I began at Walt Disney World in 1993 as director of sports development. My view had nothing to do with the fact that my parents never took me and my brothers on a vacation to any of the Disney properties as we grew up in Flint (at least not consciously). And no way was I simply hating on the Mouse.

No, this was merely the foundation of my vision. Authenticity was the ticket.

Look at it this way: Surveys showed this huge percentage of kids—like 40 percent—who don't love Mickey and hardly desired a trip to Magic Kingdom. They would never give up their passion for sports, whether it was softball, basketball, soccer, Pop Warner football, volleyball, or whatever they enjoyed athletically, to become a theme-park consumer if they had to choose one over the other. For kids who competed, sports represented their alpha and omega.

That love of athletics was what we needed to tap into as we launched our business. It needed to be about the sports, which is why it was so significant that the Amateur Athletic Union (AAU) became our first major partner in striking a deal to move its national headquarters to Wide World of Sports. In the big picture, the complex—built on more than 200 acres of what was once swampland in Osceola County on the outskirts of Orlando—supplied the theme parks with millions of visitors over the years who might otherwise have never been in the vicinity. It was an incremental audience, where people extended their visits to the sports tournaments and camps to the theme parks and stayed at the resorts. But the undeniable hook was in the athletic realm.

The facilities are still amazing, including a 7,500-seat baseball stadium (expanded with lawn seating to a capacity topping

10,000), an 8,000-seat arena, a fieldhouse, a track-and-field complex, and upwards of twenty multipurpose fields. This, in addition to the five golf courses that existed before the birth of Wide World of Sports. On top of the AAU, original tenants included the U.S. Men's Clay Court Championships, the Harlem Globetrotters, the NFL Experience, and the Atlanta Braves, who held spring training there (and broke the franchise's spring attendance record in the first year) for more than two decades.

So the participants had a broad spectrum of offerings, from amateur events to the training of elite, world-class athletes, like those on the U.S. national soccer teams, for example. Or the NFL's Tampa Bay Buccaneers and NBA's Orlando Magic. My old team, the Bengals, even held a couple of passing camps there.

It quickly became the ultimate sports destination it was intended to be, which redefined the sports complex business. Before Wide World of Sports, there were only two multisport complexes in the entire United States. There are hundreds of sports complexes now, with many municipalities staging events—marathons, soccer tournaments, baseball tournaments, basketball tournaments—to drive business.

It took two years for the corporate powers at Disney to approve my vision, allocating $220 million in 1995 to launch the project. That's the most capital any African-American had ever been granted by corporate America. Even Bob Johnson, the first African-American billionaire, didn't begin with that type of investment when he co-founded Black Entertainment Television (BET) in 1979.

On one hand, the approval process involved selling and educating people on the differentiation between our business versus the make-believe world of Magic Kingdom. I had to prove something that they didn't accept before, because they were experts on kids. Who's not going to be an expert on kids while running the "Happiest Place on Earth"? And these were the same people telling me how to launch and brand my business. That's why I recommended the hiring of Reggie Whitehead, whom I knew from Cincinnati, where he worked at Kings Island amusement park. A marketing whiz, he became the first African-American vice president at Walt Disney World, just to support my business. As he began to successfully brand our business, *I* got promoted to VP.

The philosophical battle was just the beginning. I believe that you can't fake authenticity. To get corporate approval, we obviously had to show the projected profits. As I studied it, I realized that families would take several vacations per year to support their kids' travel for sports events. That's why it was so important to have the credibility, the authenticity, at Walt Disney World, because at the time a so-called "Mickey Mouse event" was considered a negative. For entrance to a competition, someone may have paid twenty bucks, but they had to stay at a hotel, which cost them, say, $95 per night, and they might buy two theme park tickets, which meant another $150. All of a sudden, they've spent several hundred bucks on top of a $20 admission to enter our sports event.

There were several projected businesses within the Disney universe seeking financial backing. The only businesses that got approved expected the biggest returns, which we would call the "Hurdle Rate." What is your hurdle? How much return on investment (ROI) for every dollar in your business? Our starting point wasn't zero; our starting point was what Disney could make with money that was just sitting in the bank. You've got to project a return of close to 10 percent just to start. Then, your projected ROI was compared against other proposed businesses throughout the company that were also competing for those same available dollars. Part of the corporate structure at Disney is set up in an adversarial manner. There's always someone whose job it is to challenge your assumptions.

But ultimately, our business would return somewhere around 500 percent on investment. What's the business—rebranded in 2010 as the ESPN Wide World of Sports Complex—worth now? I speculate a billion, which is about what you'd pay for a good NBA franchise or a low-revenue NFL franchise these days. The reason is because of the incrementality. It's now been institutionalized, but incrementality equated to the millions of people that we brought to Walt Disney World who ended up spending money. It drove the company to strategically build and invest in a line of lower-priced, on-property Disney hotels catering to the $100 to $120 per night market for families looking for housing while at sporting events. While on-property, you get all the perks, including transportation by bus or tram. It became a huge, billion-dollar benefit for the Walt Disney World bottom line. Not only were we selling registrations for whatever event they were attending, we were selling merchandise for the event, providing the kind of attendance that drives sponsorships and bolsters food and beverage revenue. When we began Wide World of Sports, there were no businesses driving incremental attendance in that fashion at the theme parks. Disney had positioned, marketed, and branded itself so well that the people who wanted to come Walt Disney World were already coming. Especially those who'd prioritized that it would be a part of their children's memories. We significantly added to that.

And the sports business is continuing to grow at Disney. It is still adding assets, like an arena specifically for dance, continuing to drive more attendance. It steadily exceeded its pro forma in terms of return on investment. It's one of the best returns on investment that the company has achieved. Yet, in some ways, it has also moved in a different direction than when I was there. It's quote-unquote, "less authentic."

Now they can afford to be less authentic because they have hundreds of authentic sports events that they've created themselves. The three-day marathon, for instance, generates millions in profit. In that way, our business was institutionalized.

Back to Mickey. The characters were always allowed in the preexisting businesses—the water parks and golf courses—that ultimately came under my umbrella in 1997 when they created a new division and promoted me to vice president of sports and recreation. We had "Golf Mickey," which was a money-maker. I created another logo that didn't include Golf Mickey, but I still sold the Golf Mickey stuff. I'm a businessman, okay? But ultimately, over time, there was a market for a non-Mickey Mouse Disney logo that had more authenticity and spoke more to the fact that we had PGA Tour events that took place on a competitive course. It was not a Mickey Mouse course. You accomplished something if you played at this course, and you accomplished even more if you played at all five of our courses.

The grand opening of Wide World of Sports was March 28, 1997, and featured a spring training game between the Atlanta Braves and the Cincinnati Reds before a sellout crowd of more than 10,000. Deion Sanders, playing for the Reds (and the Dallas Cowboys that year too during football season), had the first hit, first stolen base, and scored the first run at the complex.

Fortunately, Braves GM John Schuerholz agreed with my authenticity principle. Turner Broadcasting—which owned the Braves and had recently merged with Time Warner—also owned Nickelodeon, which was a competitor to The Disney

Channel. Their characters were featured at Turner Field in Atlanta every now and then for Nickelodeon Days. It was easy for John and me to see eye to eye because he didn't like the Nickelodeon stuff up in Atlanta. It was, "Your characters are not allowed at my event, and my characters are not allowed at your event. We cool? Cool." We shook hands and signed it into the contract. We essentially outlawed Disney characters from Braves games and all Nickelodeon characters from Walt Disney World.

Another memory from that grand opening: Ted Turner was in our suite with his wife, Jane, when I handed him the telephone. It was Michael Eisner calling. That was the icebreaker between Turner and Disney that led to their collaborating on some things instead of expending all that energy competing with each other. These two corporate heads of state had not spoken to each other in years. It happened during that first game. That collaboration wasn't what John and I had planned when we started, but we knew it was good business.

BOOM BOX: THE PROBLEM WITH TIGER WOODS

I have a picture of my father with golfing legend Tiger Woods. It's a memory from the early days at Disney's Wide World of Sports when I hosted Tiger's first children's clinic. It was our second event after opening the complex in 1997, just before Tiger went out and won his first Masters.

We held the clinic on a soccer field at the sports complex rather than the golf course because I wanted to demonstrate that our grass was PGA-compatible—as fine as any grass you'd find on the best golf courses of America.

My father, Eli, was an avid golfer. He introduced himself to Tiger, who was very aloof but at least shook his hand and turned and posed for the picture. A classic shot.

Years later, though, he provided a different snapshot as I ran our PGA tournament.

John Schuerholz, by that time Atlanta Braves president, invited me to his suite because he had Tiger and his wife in there, and pitching ace John Smoltz thought we'd get along. But Tiger wouldn't speak to me.

That was odd. Typically, there's a mutual respect demonstrated among African-Americans in such social settings. And you don't have to fly a red-black-and-green flag—for decades symbolizing black unity and liberation—to feel a connection as a minority. But Woods, the first black Master's champion, once said on *The Oprah Winfrey Show* that it bothers him to be called an African-American. He said he created his own term, *Cablinasian*, that reflected his ethnic blend of Caucasian, Black, American Indian, and Asian. Maybe his apparent distance was an intentional way to disconnect with me, a proud African-American man.

Then there was the eighteenth hole. This is a vivid memory. He had to know, because he'd played in my tournament, that I was in some position at Disney, and I was the guy giving him the check.

But as we walked from the seventeenth green to the eighteenth tee (we'd set up a private corridor underneath the stands) and I was getting ready to say hello, he gave me the cold shoulder. It was just the two of us, and he totally walked by me as if I didn't exist at all. And this was the same guy I'd spent an hour and a half with in Schuerholz's suite. *And* I'm the guy with the check.

> It made me think: This brother doesn't have a red-black-and-green card.

Business is always connected to people. Yet inclusion for all types of people isn't and hasn't been so automatic in corporate America, even though it's good business to tap into the perspectives of a wide demographic in developing strategies, standards, and practices.

Like so many companies across America, Disney was sorely lacking on the diversity front—especially when it came to their leadership. While establishing and growing the business of the sports complex was always my top priority, and what I am most proud of from my fourteen-year tenure at Disney, impacting diversity was a priority on a parallel track.

It is my responsibility as an African-American man who has climbed the ladder to reflect the additional and constant layers of purpose—including providing fair opportunities for diversity and educating in a corporate environment—that so many of my white counterparts probably didn't have a clue about.

I was used to this duty. When I was the only African-American among the nine members of the Cincinnati City Council and issues adversely affected the black community, who did the people look to, to carry the banner and to provide a voice regarding their concerns? One of the flashbacks from my tenure on the council was City Hall almost being overrun by black citizens fighting eminent domain and the adverse effects expansion of the Cincinnati Zoo had on their property values. I was their only advocate. And it was rough.

Accepting that obligation is simply how I was raised. My parents taught me not to run away from issues that involved race, and I saw that firsthand as my parents fought to have my brothers and me enrolled in college-prep curriculums rather than general education tracks. I saw it when we marched for civil rights. I always had a sense—and a good one—of the significance of *Brown v. Board of Education*, which was decided the year I was born, 1954.

Think about the *Disney Traditions* film that I previously mentioned. With diversity of thought among key decision-makers—and a willingness to object—there would have been a sensitivity to weigh the relevance and context of having Al Jolson singing "Mammy" in blackface on the screen. Disney eventually took those images out of the film and, furthermore, created a diversity department that made other significant changes.

For some of the classic movies on Disney+, viewers are warned of "outdated cultural depictions" in a disclaimer at the end of plot descriptions. That describes exactly what I ran into with *Traditions*. It's good that Disney has responded and come to terms with some of the stereotypes it has perpetuated. That's one reason they are the top entertainment company. Their growth on diversity and in accepting new ideas, new solutions, and new partnerships has been so progressive. Obviously, I'm not taking any credit for that. But I did my part.

My department was known for being the most diverse business unit at Walt Disney World. No other department even came close. We had more women, more Hispanics, and more African-Americans than any other division. I was trying to be proactive. You have to be.

I made no apologies for what I was trying to accomplish, which is why I posted pennants in the training room that represented the number and diversity of schools where our athletic trainers came from. There were lots of opportunities for women and lots of opportunities for minorities.

A quick sidebar regarding the thinking associated with our athletic trainers, which flowed with the attention to detail that permeated our business. We set out to establish the best and most diverse internship program in the country for athletic trainers. When you went to Walt Disney World as an athletic trainer, it wasn't like in college when you're assigned to a certain sport or designated to take care of all the women athletes. There are very few training regimens in the country where someone will work with athletes from age five to ninety, in forty different sports, and bear witness to all the different injuries that can occur. And the skill set that I emphasized was that these athletic trainers also had to have phenomenal bedside manner. They might be helping a kid who was away from home without their parents, maybe for the first time, and are scared because they're hurt. That's why the Disney difference, in this case, was for our trainers to have great bedside manner.

The first head athletic trainer I hired, Drew Graham, went on to become the head athletic trainer for the NBA's Memphis Grizzlies. I knew Graham from his previous work as an assistant athletic trainer with the Bengals, and he is just one of the many people who received opportunities with us that helped us establish our proficiency as a business while allowing them to grow within their own careers.

You know Charles Davis, the college and pro football broadcaster for Fox Sports and the NFL Network? He got his start in broadcasting with us. He was always a great people person and worked for us as director of the PGA tourney, among other roles. Anytime we had VIPs on site, Charles would handle it. Maybe that's why Clint Eastwood tried to hire him away to work at Pebble Beach. And then I started the

Disney Spirit Award recognizing the most inspirational college football player, which we presented on the college football awards show that was held at Walt Disney World and broadcast by ESPN. The first two years, I made the presentations, but I had to ad-lib the second time when I couldn't read the teleprompter that was way in the back. The next day, I called Charles into my office and told him he would be the presenter the following year. Now he's one of the best broadcasters in the business.

Jeff Blake, the former Bengals quarterback, was our first intern. We had just gotten our business approved and were in the process of moving into our office space in the old office for the Animal Kingdom theme park when he came aboard. To justify my salary and scope, I had to take on other businesses—the golf business, the two water parks, and miniature golf—so Jeff was used in a variety of ways. He was with the Bengals at the time but worked for us during the offseason. Jeff is from Sanford, right outside of Orlando, so he would have been in Florida anyway. I just wanted him to lend his confident leadership persona. The fact that he was a diverse leader made it even better. He signed a $5 million contract extension with the Bengals while interning with us, which also provided me with a motivational punch line to use with our other interns: "Unless you're getting a $5 million contract, you're not working hard enough."

I have a lot of pride too whenever I see some black skin in the Olympics in the swimming events. I hired the lifeguards for our water parks and wanted diversity. I ultimately told the YMCA Aquatic Center, right off International Drive in Orlando, that I would only continue hiring from them if they started presenting some diverse candidates. It took years, but finally they started developing a pipeline.

Diversity, you see, is a byproduct of the intent to diversify. And to educate.

One of my good friends from the Disney years is Lee Cockerell, the now-retired executive vice president of operations at Disney and author of multiple bestselling books flowing from the Disney magic. I learned a great deal from Lee. He's a time-management guru. He was a great resource who helped me align my vision within the Disney environment. One reason he was there as my boss was to rein in this guy who had been rabble-rousing a little bit about the company's diversity program before he'd even started his own business.

Yet it went both ways. I taught Lee things that he didn't know. He's from Tulsa, Oklahoma, but he didn't know a thing about the Tulsa race riot in 1921, when a mob of whites terrorized black residents and businesses as they burned down the Greenwood District of the city. It is considered the worst incident of racial violence in American history, wiping out the wealthiest black community in the United States at the time, which was known as "Black Wall Street." Coming from Tulsa, you would think that Lee would have known about it. He's learned a lot about the riots since. I was able to teach him something. I earned a degree of respect with that, and he increased his interest learning more about diversity.

Members of my leadership group knew intimately of my passion in this regard. Every year, I had a team-building event. And every year, I would show a documentary of the Truth and Reconciliation Commission in South Africa that Archbishop Desmond Tutu had championed. The video is called *Long Night's Journey into Day*. Back then, I showed it on a VHS tape. The story revolves around four acts of forgiveness—four different scenarios of unforgivable sins that people found ways to forgive. If I watched the video now, seeing black mothers forgiving a black police officer for ambushing and killing their kids at the behest of the racist white apartheid regime, I'd cry. Four mothers. And they all refused, initially, to even consider the concept of forgiveness in these situations.

If I had a person in our group who didn't cry, I would wonder why, and I'd talk to them about it. I talked to everyone about it because I wanted to know what their experiences were. Even those in our organization who'd seen the film three or four times. It changes your demeanor.

The ability to forgive is one of the toughest human traits. Disney does a great job of teaching hospitality, but part of really being committed to someone's happiness is having empathy rather than being condescending. In order for me to have an authentic business, it was important for every aspect of my organization to have authentic empathy.

That's why Lee and I have the kind of relationship we have. He considers me a son, and he is someone I'd consider a second father. Empathy is part of that equation.

The willingness for me to go there is inherent to my leadership. Sure, I was the manager who began meetings with a mantra that began with me saying, "Failure…" which prompted the group to respond, "…is not an option." It was ingrained.

My leadership, though, was anything but dictatorial. It was team-oriented. I'd like to think the reason that I dominated in company-wide ratings of executives by staffers—in a company known for having great leaders—was because I never treated people who worked under me as if I was better than they were. It was important to not only carry myself with an enthusiasm that I believe is contagious, but also to provide a sense to the staff that our mission included improving the quality of their lives.

The challenge at Disney was similar to that with the Cincinnati City Council in that I had so much to learn about things

I had never been exposed to in order to be effective. When I signed on, I never would have thought I'd have any passion for running a water park. But you know what? I loved it. I had to learn about water chemicals and how to keep guests safe in it. I had to learn about lifeguarding. I had to learn about how to prevent anything bad from happening. That meant taking care of food in a hot area versus secured environments. Dealing with sand. Dealing with wildlife that visit 24/7. So many different things: the look; the brand; the experience of our guests; the ratings of our guests; the hospitality of our cast. And these things are different in a water park than on a golf course. In a water park, guests expect all these experiences. On a golf course, they paid $125 and expected an entirely different, more personalized, experience.

It turned out that Disney provided me one of the most personally rewarding experiences of my life. The net result of all the decisions resulted in a successful business that went through a lot of growing pains. But because the vision was solid—a vision that I brought to the table—it's still a thriving, evolving business under the leadership of Maribeth Bisienere.

Sharp vision, conscientious leadership, and bottom-line success are surely elements of a winning combination. But that certainly did not insulate me from certain risks and threats that came with big business. It's a dog-eat-dog world, you know, full of alpha dogs. Two cases that involved some very high-profile people underscored that.

Let's start with Mark McCormack. The late founder of International Management Group (IMG) essentially attempted to take my business away from me when it was in its infancy. McCormack invited me along with Bud Dare, who was in charge of all Disney's third-party vendors, to a meeting at his house in Islesworth, near Orlando. At that point, IMG operated one of the two or three multisport complexes in the country, but they were primarily into tennis. I didn't know what McCormack wanted. I thought the meeting, if anything, was going to help us. About how he could be a resource, as opposed to what I found him to be.

We were sitting on his patio, by the pool, overlooking one of the lakes in Islesworth. Bud was there to possibly advance McCormack's proposal to his bosses—who were not the people I reported to but who still had the power to replace me. Well, McCormack proposed to Bud Dare—after *I'd* gotten the business approved—that IMG was better suited to build the event calendar for Wide World of Sports than Reggie Williams, whose idea it was in the first place. This was a face-to-face meeting, and he was telling one of my bosses why he and his organization were better than I was. And I had to sit there, act professionally, nod, and be respectful because he was a major player in the industry. But there was no way I was going to let him usurp my business.

He was very aggressive. And if someone is going to be that aggressive, you'd rather it be face-to-face. That's what I was used to on the football field. But I felt so disrespected by Mark McCormack. In the end, he notched another chip on my shoulder and was another reason why I was so determined to be successful in growing our business.

Ultimately, instead of us mimicking IMG's business model, IMG mimicked Wide World of Sports. They started expanding into more sports and events. Our calendar was robust. When I retired from the business in 2007 after more than ten years, we were doing close to 225 events per year. We had already exceeded our pro forma, which was 140 events. And unlike the IMG model, we didn't make Celebration High School a "super school" like Montverde Academy or IMG Academy, which recruited prime athletes from across the nation to fuel their programs and essentially played a travel-team schedule. Given the potential PR issues with that, on top of the costs of housing athletes and the slippery slope of recruiting, we chose not to use that approach.

The other case involved famed attorney Johnnie Cochran, who cross-examined me during a civil trial that resulted in a jury handing Disney a $240 million loss that was eventually appealed and amended through an undisclosed settlement.

That was one of the most acrimonious scenarios that I ever walked into, stemming from an issue that originated years earlier while I was playing in the NFL. Apparently, the two plaintiffs—one of whom was a former minor league umpire fired for stealing baseballs—came up with some idea for a sports complex and took it to people at Walt Disney World. When we announced that we were doing the sports complex, the ump and his associates sued, claiming we had stolen their idea. Yet I had developed the whole thing. Disney's argument was that the idea of a sports complex was too generic. The lawsuit was thrown out, but a couple of years later, after we opened, they filed another lawsuit with Willie Gary as the lead attorney... aligned with Cochran. They culled the jury. Once they eliminated all the people who didn't like Johnnie Cochran and all the people who were positive about Disney, the jury pool was not a good one for Walt Disney World. It ended up being a five-week trial. I was the face of Disney...and the last witness.

We were wronged. We utilized no part of this other party's intelligence in any way, shape, or form. There wasn't anything that we borrowed or that we stole. Everything that we decided to include in the sports complex was meticulously derived by study. Bob Glinka had done a lot of the nuts-and-bolts work. My job was to drive the vision.

The night before I went on the stand, I got a call from Wallace Ford, the lawyer who introduced me to Cochran years earlier when we'd all had lunch in New York. I didn't accept his calls on the first two attempts, then picked up to hear him maintain that he had "heard from [their] legal team" and that Gary's cross-examination would not be acrimonious because they respected me. That was total crapola. They pulled the switcheroo and had Cochran cross-examine me. It was totally unexpected. Ford's call had been camouflage for Cochran. And Johnnie came after me. He demeaned football players. He used racial stereotypes against me. It really pissed me off. He tried to make the point that I couldn't have figured out this whole business by myself because my pro forma maintained, among a myriad of details, that we could broadcast a marathon. The way that you broadcast a marathon is with a drone. Now, that's common knowledge, but at the time it wasn't. Cochran ridiculed the idea. He didn't know that I had spent time among the military—when I was with the World League of American Football, our training camp was at Patrick Air Force Base in Florida—and was familiar with how drones could be utilized.

Our general counsel thought I did a great job. He said, "You were a mensch!" (That's Yiddish for a person of integrity and honor.) He thought I'd saved the company a quarter of a billion bucks, but we still had a $240 million judgment levied against us. After I left the courtroom in downtown Orlando, I just drove around for two hours, trying to figure out what I was going to do to save the business. At that point in time, Disney didn't have any loyalty. It was all about the bottom line.

As it turned out, I would have bigger, more personal issues to deal with.

CHAPTER 11
INVICTUS

I'M LYING IN A HOSPITAL BED, UNABLE TO SPEAK.

The day after being stricken by a stroke, I regained the feeling that had been lost on the entire right side of my body, aided by the clot-busting drugs administered in the emergency room. I had movement in my arm and leg, sensations that again matched the other side of my body.

But I still couldn't talk. I could think the sounds, but I could not enunciate. I couldn't give the hospital staff my Social Security number. Couldn't give them my son's phone number. Couldn't provide any information about my insurance coverage.

This was New Year's Day of 2016 in Punta Gorda, Florida. What a horrible way to christen the start of another year. I was so frustrated. I had assumed that with the clot-busters, I'd wake up and ta-da! But the next morning, I still couldn't talk.

Because there were no rooms available at the hospital, they'd created a makeshift solution for me by cordoning off a part of the post-op recovery area for me to have a bed. I was there with the doctor and the nurses, trying to say things to the doctor to no avail. In that moment, the frustration of not being able to speak and articulate after my stroke exceeded all of the frustration with all of my various physical injuries. It was probably what people feel when dealing with Parkinson's or Lou Gehrig's disease. Feeling mentally trapped inside your mind and being unable to break out of that trap was like what I later saw in the Jordan Peele horror movie *Get Out*, when the main character awakens strapped to a chair in a darkened basement.

Then, all of a sudden, I thought: "Invictus."

It's the classic poem that William Ernest Henley began writing in 1873 at an infirmary in England while trying to save his leg from amputation. It's what Nelson Mandela repeatedly recited while being held captive for twenty-seven years, eighteen of them in a prison on Robben Island off the coast of Cape Town. And it was the poem I learned word for word at Dartmouth College to become a fraternity brother of Alpha Phi Alpha.

In one of the worst predicaments of my existence, "Invictus" flowed off my tongue.

Out of the night that covers me,
Black as the pit from pole to pole,
I thank whatever gods may be
For my unconquerable soul.

In the fell clutch of circumstance
I have not winced nor cried aloud.
Under the bludgeoning of chance
My head is bloody, but unbowed.

Beyond this place of wrath and tears
Looms but the horror of the shade,

INVICTUS

And yet the menace of the years
Finds, and shall find me, unafraid.

It matters not how strait the gate,
How charged with punishments the scroll,
I am the master of my fate:
I am the captain of my soul.

The doctor began clapping. The nurses and all the patients in their own areas did too. Suddenly everyone was cheering. I was able to talk again. It's one of those life lessons. You are going to learn things that can save your life or put you in a position to lose it. It was apropos that "Invictus" was the trigger to regaining my speech.

I have lived an "Invictus" life.

The stroke occurred less than two years after I'd undergone an aortic dissection. The doctor initially refused to proceed with the heart operation until I provided him with contact information for my next of kin because he feared that I was on the verge of death. It was several years after I underwent nine surgeries over the course of five weeks in a New York City hospital, when the amputation of my right leg was an option that collided head-on with my intense desire to save it. The new crisis came a little more than a decade after my bilateral knee replacement—that's both knees—that was later plagued by complications including a life-threatening bone infection that was contained only after enduring seven excruciating biopsies to facilitate the treatment.

That's merely a slice of the serious issues I've encountered, physically and emotionally, that have forced me to draw on and appreciate the resilience at the core of my existence.

Bottom line: I'm still here to tell it. I'm a survivor, a fighter, a determined soul who has been to hell and back. I'm still here for a reason. Or for several reasons that represent the human spirit.

The word *invictus*, translated from Latin, means "unconquerable." Yeah, that's me. Clearly, I have long realized, even without my brushes with death, that, as humans, none of us is totally invincible. But I also know that you can never willingly give up. Others will give up on you, write you off, consider you finished. Yet the opinions of others have little to do with your foundation of hope. Those other voices are merely a nuisance, unless you allow them to become more.

Basically, I am my own Bundini. You know who Bundini is? That's Drew "Bundini" Brown, Muhammad Ali's cornerman. He was the one in the corner telling Ali, "You're the greatest, man! No one can beat you! You float like a butterfly and sting like a bee!"

You've got to be your own Bundini, like: "I've got this pain. I can work this out." You've got to be confident to come to grips with failure and challenges. You've got to train yourself to see the positive solution. That's at the core of living "Invictus." It starts with the mind.

Let me share a tale of two nurses. This coincided with my release from the Hospital for Special Surgery in New York City on September 18, 2008—I remember the date because my birthday is September 19, and I can't be in the hospital on my birthday—when they had to cauterize some more of the area in my knee that had become dead tissue during the process of saving my leg. They had to put tubes into my disfigured leg. I left the hospital around eight o'clock that night. Well, on the cab ride home, one of those things dislodged. I'm thinking, "Do I tell the cab driver to turn around and take me back to the hospital or not?" I wanted to stay out of the hospital. I went to my room, which was in a new apartment building that my

Alpha frat brother, Steve White, had found for me, while all my operations were taking place. I had run out the lease at the other place that he found for me. The next morning, I slept in. But I was worried about my leg, so, I set up two home visits from nurses.

The first was a male nurse. His job was to deal with my PICC (peripherally inserted central catheter) line. He was checking everything with the PICC line, but he kept looking at my leg. By protocol, he's not supposed to touch any other part of my body, but he said, "Look, man. I can help your leg. Let me re-bandage it." I said, "Please. Please." So, he re-bandaged it professionally, then he left.

That afternoon, I was feeling better. I was doing an interview for the *New York Times* with George Vecsey when the second nurse, a white female, came in. Her job was to bandage my knee, which wasn't looking as bad as it had a few hours earlier because of the first nurse. But she un-bandaged it and said, "Ugh, man! That's the ugliest knee I've ever seen!"

I was taken aback. She said, "So ugly!"

I said, "Wait a minute, hold up. I think it's the most beautiful knee that I've ever seen because this is where it came from."

Just like beauty is in the eye of the beholder, so is ugly if that's what you choose to see.

I showed her some of the pictures that documented my knee's surgical journey, complete with open gaps and blood and stuff. She quickly backtracked and concluded, "Wow, it *is* beautiful."

That's when my whole mentality changed. From then on, I was going to aggressively defend the looks of my knee rather than thinking I had ugliness on my body. That mentality, that switch, that commitment, has driven everything since, because it has all been for a good reason: saving my leg.

Where has that knee been? I thought the bilateral knee replacement, performed by Dr. Steve O'Brien in October 2005 at the Hospital for Special Surgery, had gone perfectly. I went back to my career as vice president of sports attractions at Walt Disney World with the most significant lingering issues from my fourteen years as an NFL linebacker surgically addressed. The right knee was the problem, the one for which, during the 1980s, I underwent guinea-pig abrasion surgery, the forerunner to microfracture surgery.

Because I was born bow-legged, I had to have both knees replaced. You can't have one curved leg and one straight leg. Prosthetics are always straight. My left leg was the sacrificial lamb to fix the damage in my right knee. After the surgeries, I gained an inch in height. The hip, though, suddenly hurt more than the knee. But the net result was that I could walk better!

A few months later, though, that euphoria morphed into a new level of grief.

I became ill on the eve of Super Bowl XL in Detroit, where I stayed at the Renaissance Center, the riverfront hotel that was the NFL's headquarters that week. I had dinner that evening with Soulan Johnson, a former girlfriend I had run into, at Seldom Blues, the upscale restaurant in the hotel owned by former Detroit Lions star Robert Porcher. We had a great meal. About midnight, though, I awakened to heaves and was throwing up worse than I ever had in my life. I went to see the NFL doctor at the hotel, and he thought it was probably food poisoning. He gave me some antibiotics and sent me on my way. He had no idea what I came to believe it really was—a root canal that I'd had done twenty-five years earlier which had become infected. They used to use silver "points" as a filling material, only to discover that after a certain period, they would become infected. I had a mouth infection that migrated to the other, weakest part of my body—my right knee.

At that time, the rehab on my left knee was done, and I had 120 degrees range of motion. The right knee had a range of 113 to 115 degrees. I could have been happily satisfied, after the fact, with the limits of motion on one leg versus the other. But I wanted it to be perfect. While working to improve the knee through physical therapy, I was tearing scar tissue. That's how it became the weakest point that the infection migrated to.

I had no idea how bad things was. If I had gotten the right antibiotics immediately, probably through a PICC line, maybe they could have killed the bug before it infiltrated so deeply into my knee. Who really knows? All I know is that the antibiotics the NFL doctor gave me helped. I felt better the next morning. My chest hurt from all the heaving, but I was able to enjoy the game. But by the next day, I didn't have any more antibiotics, and my knee was really hurting as I hobbled to the plane bound for Orlando. I went straight to a meeting at Epcot Center that Monday morning and could barely walk. Then things really took a bad turn. I went to the hospital and was told that I had a raging infection and that they needed to admit me immediately to take out the infected prosthetic. I had never met the doctor, Kenneth Krumins, who performed the surgery.

This went down the day before we launched the World Baseball Classic with a game between Puerto Rico and Cuba at our pristine stadium at Disney's Wide World of Sports. It was an international showcase that I'd worked on for over a year. It was going to be at our place, my little baby. But Dr. Krumins told me surgery was needed immediately.

When I woke after the surgery to remove the prosthetic, it was like hot acid had been poured into the incision. At that point in time, it was the worst pain I'd experienced in my life.

Obviously, since then I've had worse. Compounding that, he replaced the prosthetic with one that went from mid-femur to mid-tibia, and he hadn't told me he was going to do that. Not only was it much heavier, it chopped away a lot of femur. I lost three inches of length in my leg. That was such a pain.

They asked me to get up the day after surgery. That's always the big mystery: Can you do it? I got up, went into the shower, turned on the hot water, and just cried, cried, cried. Not because of the pain but because of the worst-case scenario of missing the World Classic. It was on TV; I could watch it from my room, but in my mind, it was an unfair stroke of fortune that I couldn't be there.

After the surgery, they put me on a four-month regimen of an antibiotic that, according to blood tests, had cured me of my bone infection, osteomyelitis. They implanted another knee. I rehabbed again. But from 2006 until the end of 2007, I was rehabbing a wound that wouldn't close. There was always one spot oozing. That means you've got a problem.

Part of the problem was that the infection wasn't cured. Krumins dropped me as a patient in 2007 as he dealt with his own health issues. He said my problems were too big for him. They were over his head. He wound up leaving his profession for a while too.

I turned back to O'Brien, which led to repeated trips to New York for seven agonizing biopsy procedures over four months as we sought an antidote to the infection. The invasive procedure involved scraping my knee to extract a culture of bacteria. This, without anesthetic. It was a big ol' needle, and they were trying to get as much of a sample as possible to grow the bug in a laboratory. The first five times, it didn't work. It worked on the sixth. Then they needed another sample to confirm the results. The seventh procedure was the worst one.

They couldn't get anything. He really had to scrape my knee until he finally got enough material to put on little lab glass plates. That was some drama.

He had this big needle in my knee, trying to get any kind of suction. He was moving it all around, and the nurse who witnessed this almost got sick to her stomach. Sticking a needle in a joint is painful as heck. Finally, the doctor got a little bit of the necessary sample.

He said, "Go get a screen!" Usually, they would have a test tube or something like that. If he got enough to at least get on a screen, a glass slide, he might be able to save it. That girl—*whoosh!*—she sprinted out of my room like the Roadrunner. She had to go to another floor. She was back in a couple of minutes, but the whole time that she was gone, this big ass needle was stuck in my knee. I couldn't move it. I was grateful at that point that Steve was also a friend because our conversation took my mind off the needle.

The nurse came back with the slide. Steve took it and said, "Oh, but I need two." She took off again—*whoosh!*—same cartoon. She came back, and he got just enough on one slide and everything else on the second slide. Once they confirmed the osteomyelitis, they admitted me within the week—just enough time for me to fly home then drive back to New York from Orlando.

That was in April 2008, four months after I retired from Disney. When your health issues become more critical than your job on a constant basis, you must make a decision. Not that it was an easy decision for someone who'd spent his football career fighting through one injury after another, conditioned to play with pain. I loved my job. It was my vision realized. We were doing close to 225 events per year, which was an indication of our growth. But I couldn't walk anymore. I was unable to walk the talk. My last two years there—and everyone knew this—I'd ice my legs during meetings. It was a distraction. I was running a business. When the people who are working for you are more concerned about your health than the health of the business, you've got to go. Or, at least in my mind, it was time to go.

Besides, I needed to devote my full attention to my health. Shortly after arriving in New York, I experienced the worst pain of my life—the night that I awakened from the dream where I went to hell to retrieve my dear friend Lenny Nichols from the clutches of Satan.

After that, it was another round with a PICC line—four more months of antibiotics delivered intravenously through the jugular—to fight the infection. I was treated with Vancomycin, which at the time was a new, really strong antibiotic. The medication takes over your immune system, providing all of the white blood cell immunity properties. Your body can quit making white blood cells itself if you're on it for too long. That's always the risk.

Once I got off the PICC line, I was put on oral antibiotics. Apparently, they prescribed the wrong antibiotics because they basically neutralized my white-cell count. My doctor called with a grim message:

"You need to come in now because your immune system has gone kaput," he said. "You do not have any white blood cells. You need to get off the streets of New York before you get sick."

I said, "I'll be in tomorrow. I want to spend one last night in my own bed."

And one more night getting high. Getting prepared. Because suddenly, I had another crisis.

When I returned to the hospital, they put me in reverse quarantine. I was kept in a room, and everyone who came in contact with me dressed in protective gear. It was one of the worst moments of the ordeal. I had nine operations in five months—an embolization, removal of the infected knee, four abrasion procedures to remove dead tissue, two gastric flap surgeries, and the final knee replacement—but being in reverse quarantine really makes you feel like a reject of society. At the time, the only thing they could do if you lost your immune system was to administer an injection from a class of drugs called CSFs—colony stimulating factors—which boost cell production. It was just one shot, and they said it would take about twenty-four hours to see if it would work. After an injection of Neupogen, I slept the best that I could.

When I awoke the next morning, the first thing I saw on my smartphone was a letter from Desmond Tutu. The sense of destiny with this letter? I had not had any contact with Archbishop Tutu in more than a dozen years, since seeing him at the '96 Olympics in Atlanta. Lee Cockerell, my boss at Disney and still a very close friend, had run into Tutu and told him what I was going through. That's why Tutu sent me the letter that read:

Dear Reggie,

Your friends Lee and Priscilla sent a press cutting to a friend who forwarded it me.

What an awful situation with your knee. I am so sorry to hear about your present suffering and give thanks for the joy you brought many with your scintillating play in your heyday, but especially for your support of our anti-apartheid struggle. Today we are free and Democratic and it is in large measure due to the support we got from (people) such as yourselves. Thank you for your contribution.

We want to wish you well over all the surgeries and that you will recover fully.

God bless you richly,

Desmond Tutu.

It was uplifting. And the timing made it incredibly special. After I saw Tutu's letter, the doctors came into my room, administered a test, and proclaimed: "Your immune system is back!" My white blood cell count had returned twelve hours ahead of schedule.

Ultimately, the knee was replaced again. It was the fulcrum from which other attempts to save my leg from amputation exist. Yet other challenges persisted.

Unlike the knee issues, which represented ongoing battles that extended back to the early stages of my NFL career, other health crises seemingly came out of nowhere to test my "Invictus" spirit.

One morning in 2014, I put myself through stretching exercises like always. Stretching was a measure to combat the pain that had existed since the bilateral knee replacement and the subsequent procedure that resulted in my right leg being three inches shorter than the left. I felt misaligned from my shoulder to the knee. I could feel the parts moving together. Part of my goal was to straighten out the right leg and the hip where the epicenter of discomfort was. That's why I woke up every morning having to stretch, stretch, stretch.

Well, I was stretching and twisting and suddenly something tore. I felt it in my stomach. A hot shower didn't help. I checked my temperature and other things, but after about an hour, I still didn't feel right and decided to go to the hospital. Wobbling, I couldn't drive. I called Jonathan, a brother who worked in my building as the superintendent. Jonathan was my guy. He told me to meet him at the second-floor elevator and he'd drive me to the hospital. Before I could even close the door after getting in his car, I had these rapid-fire expulsions of vomit. My internal organs were shutting down. Jonathan called 911. The EMTs stabilized me as the ambulance headed to Florida Hospital in Winter Park.

After a series of X-rays, they discovered the entire length of my aorta was torn and bleeding. If it wasn't fixed within twenty-four hours, I wouldn't live. But they didn't have a doctor available. They considered flying me to another hospital under the Florida Hospital umbrella—Shands Hospital in Gainesville—where there was a cardiologist who could do the open-heart surgery. Then they did something that I give them a lot of professional credit for: They called the competition. They contacted Orlando Regional, seeking an available surgeon. Fortunately, and in more ways than one, Dr. Mark Sand, head of the cardiology department, was available. I was whisked to the regional trauma center with sirens wailing.

Sand advised me of the severity of the situation and the critical time factor as I bled internally while we talked. He asked for the phone number of my next of kin. I'm thinking, "Nah, there's no need to call anyone." It was ten or eleven at night. I said I didn't want him to call my mom or dad, wake them up, and scare them; I didn't want him to call any of my family. But he insisted.

He said, "You don't have a choice. You're about to die. And I'm going to call your next of kin."

He demanded that I give him my mother's phone number and my son's phone number. My mom was my next of kin, but the only one in town was my son Julien. When I finally gave the doctor their numbers, he admitted me. They wheeled me off and prepped me for surgery.

Julien came quickly. Dr. Sand also called my mom and explained everything. My mom takes bad news well. It's probably the training that comes in dealing with at-risk kids that she was recognized for. As the doctor told her about my peril, she told him about my father, whose kidneys were failing and who refused to see more doctors. He had basically given up.

Well, Dr. Sand had a son at the University of Michigan Medical School. He said, "I'll have my son go up there to convince him to see a renal doctor and start dialysis." He talked to my mom for about twenty minutes. Afterward, she convinced my father to start seeing another doctor. He lived another three or four years because of that. But the bedside manner of a doctor speaking to someone he didn't know and having that type of interpersonal compassion was so impressive. That was my doctor, Dr. Sand.

When your sternum gets cut, they basically put your body on a rack as they're doing the repair. They're keeping your heart going, hooked to a machine with other organs, but the rest of your body is limp, hanging to facilitate the blood flow while they are operating on the heart. My procedure took six hours. When they put my sternum back together, they inserted a titanium bar with four screws, two on each side of the incision that extended from my throat to my stomach.

When I woke after surgery, the first person I saw was Julien. I was in an observation room, with a window where he could see in and I could see out. I was on my back. As I opened my eyes and focused, they went straight to him. That was the first thing I remembered since the previous night when I discussed the surgery with Dr. Sand before they put me under and prepped me for surgery. I saw Julien for an instant, then dozed right back to sleep.

Later that morning, after they moved me to a post-op room, I had to try to walk. I was off crutches thinking there was no way I could do it. But they insisted. I got out of bed with no idea if my leg was going to function. Before the surgery, the worst pain in my leg was not the knee; it was the hip, which served as a shock absorber because of the length disparity in my leg. That's what was so painful—grinding on the sciatic nerve. Yet somehow, having my body on the rack allowed something, somewhere, to realign itself. It wasn't perfect, but it was so much better.

The aortic dissection eliminated 80 percent of the discomfort. It was almost worth it. Almost. I was able to get off crutches. But in stretching a little bit, I popped one of the screws in the titanium bar. Now there was a screw poking through, slightly visible in my chest.

Worried, I went to the hospital. Dr. Sand said, "Do you want me to go back into your chest to pull it out and change it? The only way it will affect you is if you take any type of impact on your chest, and then it will probably go through the skin. If you fear that, I'll open you back up."

I opted to live with that screw and hope that I don't fall on my chest.

I don't take anything for granted. Like the torn heart muscle, the stroke came out of the blue to present an immediate crisis. I had moved from Orlando to Punta Gorda, along the west coast of the state, during the summer of 2015. I didn't know anyone there, but I'm a creature of habit and I'll go to the same restaurants that I like. I frequented Downtown Gatorz Bar and Grille, a sports bar that had the NFL Sunday Ticket. I'd go there to watch the Bengals play.

I had a disagreement with the owner, Doug Harris, my first time there. He disapproved of me having my leg up, resting on a chair. He didn't realize that I was nursing an injury.

"You've got your shoe off *and* your leg up?" he said.

I explained my predicament, that the leg didn't bend. He apologized—and gained a repeat customer.

Months later, Doug was the one who took me to the hospital after I suffered the stroke in his restaurant.

I was watching the Cotton Bowl on New Year's Eve—Michigan State was getting its ass kicked by Alabama—and all of a sudden, my arm started fluttering. I was alone and asked another patron, "What is going on with my arm?" He looked at me like I was crazy. The bartender came over and asked if I was okay. I told her, no, and to get Doug.

He knew the seriousness of the issue by my slurred speech. I was having a stroke. It took about ten minutes to get to the hospital, but by then I couldn't articulate anything. It was within the three-hour window needed to save stroke victims, although every minute is precious. Doug verified the timing of exactly when it happened and got me admitted.

Another life lesson: You never know who might save your life.

And the next words I spoke were from "Invictus," the ultimate reflection on my life.

BOOM BOX: NFL NEEDS TO DO BETTER FOR THOSE WHO BUILT THE GAME

It's a shame that there are two types of NFL retirees when it comes to pension benefits: those who played after 1993…and those who played before 1993.

The difference is staggering.

It's why former NFL players like myself in the pre-'93 class have spent years fighting for the type of pension parity achieved long ago by retirees in the NBA and Major League Baseball.

The median pension for someone in our class is about $30,000 per year—without healthcare coverage. For a former major leaguer who played during that same period, the pension is nearly $53,000, with a 33 percent discount to join baseball's health insurance plan. An NBA player from that period receives more than $95,000 per year plus free healthcare for life.

Thankfully, I reached my sixty-fifth birthday, allowing me to receive Medicare coverage. Before that, my monthly pension of $4,000—the amount determined by my fourteen seasons in the NFL—didn't even cover my insurance premiums. And I know NFL brethren with physical issues worse than mine who have suffered more financially than I have.

The treatment of the pre-'93 class by the NFL and NFL players union has been appalling. The pensions hardly keep up with inflation. Additional resources, such as the 88 Plan, Player Care Foundation, and Dire Need Fund, serve relatively few, with narrow standards for tapping into that assistance. And the pension increases over the years only amount to a drop in the bucket.

That's the thanks former players have gotten for sacrificing their bodies to help grow the NFL into the most popular and richest sports league in the land.

It would be better late than never for them to support the class that continues to age.

As the NFL and NFL Players Association ramped up negotiations for a new labor agreement—with both sides pledging to help the older retirees who don't have a seat at the bargaining table—a significant increase in the monthly compensation for the pre-'93 class under the Bert Bell Pension Plan loomed as one solution. That would help defray some of the significant out-of-pocket expenses that most of the players have had to pay to reach age sixty-five.

And I still think we should retroactively get 100 percent healthcare, even as there are fewer and fewer in the pre-'93 class of about 3,400 retirees as of 2019. For the players who aren't covered otherwise, the NFL and NFLPA should provide assistance as soon as possible.

On top of that, eliminating the pre-'93 class and creating pension parity with current players is the right thing to do. The post-'93 players receive an average of $58,000 per year in pension—twice as much as pre-'93 retirees—in addition to other benefits, including healthcare coverage for five years after leaving the NFL.

Both sides, NFL owners and players, pay for the retiree benefits by earmarking a small share of revenues for retirees. How much of a share is the issue.

Then there are the people that don't have any conscience in this and are not going to want to take any pay cut: agents. They control the margins but evidently don't allow for something really smart—like taking care of the pre-'93s.

This needs to change. Like yesterday.

CHAPTER 12

FAMILY

ALL THREE OF MY SONS MADE THE JUMP TO COLLEGE SPORTS as walk-ons. I am so proud of them. Julien was a state champion long jumper who took his talent to Michigan State. Jarren started out in football at Central Florida, then walked on to the wrestling team and won two national championship titles. Kellen was not only a linebacker at Vanderbilt, he was a team captain when they upset mighty Florida—which failed to recruit him out of high school.

My sons were all awarded various levels of athletic scholarships—in no small part because they earned them.

I can't help but believe this was more than a coincidence.

After all, their dad was a walk-on at Dartmouth—remember, there were no athletic scholarships in the Ivy League—after Bo Schembechler thwarted my dreams of playing football in the Big House at the University of Michigan.

I'm proud that my sons took on challenges when they weren't assured of the outcome. Anytime you're a walk-on, you're inevitably going to face rejection. Overcoming rejection, though, is a hallmark of maturity. There will be many rejections throughout our lives, but you can't be defeated before you start.

If they got that resilience from me, then I got it from my father. It was illuminated by that powerful rejection from Schembechler. Rather than allow me to wallow in self-pity, my father focused on the solution: "No matter. We'll go to Dartmouth instead."

"But Dad, I don't have a scholarship there. It's going to cost you…"

"It doesn't matter. I'll get another job."

He immediately distanced me from my biggest disappointment by finding a solution. And if I bought into what he was telling me, then I could let go of the pain.

To hear my mother, Julia, connect the dots, this is the type of resolve that has defined the Williams family for generations. The traits passed on to me from my father flowed from his father, Monroe. Of course, my mom would know. She and my father married in 1952 and barely spent a day apart for nearly sixty-seven years until his passing in 2018 after battling cancer.

Both of my grandfathers were deceased when I was born, but I have learned much about them and my family's history—on my father's side of the tree as well as my mother's—through my mother's research and detailed documentation.

What a wonderful gift she has provided for our family, much of which was crafted using notes that she took from conversations with various relatives before they passed on. This was in addition to her own observations and preservation of documents, photos, and other material. It's a framework for preserving the accomplishments of the family that grows with each generation. From the well-organized material that my mother packaged and presented to us—and through word of mouth over the years—I can tell you a lot about our history.

I'm boiling it down here, but you'll get the idea as it all relates to who I've become.

My family's name, for instance, was originally Williamson. At some point in the 1900s, Monroe dropped the "on." Imagine: Reggie Williamson.

My mother's parents came to Flint from Puerto Rico in 1925. Lucia Colon married Ines Casellas less than two weeks after she received her high school diploma in San Juan. Ines came to Michigan via Ellis Island and sent for Lucia. They had three children, including my Aunt Dalia and Uncle Admando, but Ines passed away two days before my mom's fourth birthday.

Lucia used insurance proceeds after her husband's death in 1939 to purchase a house on Grant Street, near the Buick plant on the North Side. She ultimately sent for relatives, including her mother, Mamita, to live in Flint and remarried twice.

For a short time before she worked at Buick, which manufactured tanks during World War II, Lucia received government assistance. After she landed a job working on the spark plug assembly line, she insisted on repaying the government what she had received in welfare even though it was not required. That says much about her spirit.

My affinity for learning Spanish is undoubtedly in my DNA. Mamita and Lucia, like other relatives, spoke Spanish in addition to fluent English. My mother grew up understanding Spanish but wasn't allowed to speak it. She was raised to speak English exclusively because her mother felt it was essential for being better accepted in society. The irony isn't lost on me that a generation later, I spent an entire semester immersed in Mexico learning Spanish.

My appreciation of art—people tell me that visiting my home is like going to a gallery—also traces to my mother's heritage. My Uncle Mando, who moved from Flint to New York to become a commercial artist, had a distinct influence on me. And I see it every day in the portrait of my father that was painted by Mando, hanging in my hallway.

Eli came from a much bigger family, with its roots in Livingston, Alabama. Monroe and Lula had twelve children, most of whom wound up in Flint—the migration in many of the cases stemming from a need to escape the racism of the South during the Jim Crow era.

A neat tidbit about Lula, known as "Big Mama" to her grandchildren: she was taught to preserve foods by none other than George Washington Carver.

Monroe worked for the railroads. Initially, he was a section-gang worker who laid and performed maintenance on the tracks. He later became a track walker, responsible for inspections. He and Lula were deeply spiritual. Monroe was a choir director and deacon for his Baptist church; the home he built ultimately became the nursery of his church. And to hear my Aunt Sadie—the youngest of Eli's siblings—speak about Monroe's emphasis on education is more evidence of one way my father was a chip off the old block.

"The Williamses are smart people," my Aunt Sadie said. "We like school."

My father had only one picture of Monroe. No matter. Hearing the stories, I carry a tremendous amount of respect and appreciation for what he accomplished in a life that was too short. I have always felt he was a victim of his times. His life under Jim Crow had to have been so hard. Yet the love he had for his family is apparent to me because he not only developed a big family, which was common in the black community at that time, but also a tight-knit family. That love had to have flowed from the top. When you didn't have wealth financially, you could have wealth in numbers. My knowledge of him is that he was someone who worked so hard to raise his family that he worked himself to death at fifty-two. Quite honestly, when I hear it suggested that fifty-seven is the life expectancy of an NFL player, I'm thinking the hardships I put myself through as an NFL player pale in comparison to the hardships my grandfather went through.

My father moved to Flint in 1947, fleeing from Birmingham in a fashion that is not unfamiliar to the history of many African-American families in this nation

The story I've been told—and my uncles confirmed it—is that, as part of his full-time job, my father was driving a truck to assist some of the other workers in loading the wood they were cutting down. At that time, it was basically mandated that a white person drove the truck. Well, my father knew how to drive, and it was easier on the group if someone moved the truck closer. When my father did, the foreman came and pulled him out the cab of the truck because he wasn't supposed to be driving, used the N-word, blah-blah-blah. And my father hit him. Hit him so hard that he thought he'd killed him. He and his brothers, who were also working there, immediately went home, packed up, and were on the road to Michigan the next day.

That was a sign of the times. If one brother did something, all the brothers were liable. The whole family was liable. Therefore, all the male progeny of the house headed north. This was in the '40s. There would likely be Ku Klux Klan justice served on my father for daring to hit a white man. He hadn't killed the foreman; he'd only knocked him out, but it would not be forgiven. It was, "If you let one N-word do it, you let all N-words do it." That was Alabama.

Of all the atrocities committed over so many decades across the racist Deep South, Alabama was the worst place of all—an essential police state without a conscience when it came to justice for African-Americans. In the years after my father fled, the state became the most fertile battleground of the civil rights movement, with episodes including the Montgomery Bus Boycott, the "Bloody Sunday" attack on marchers at the Edmund Pettis Bridge in Selma as they sought voting rights, and the notorious Bull Connor, the so-called "public safety commissioner" in Birmingham, who turned fire hoses and police dogs on peaceful protestors, including children. Birmingham was dubbed "Bombingham" for the routine terrorist attacks on homes, churches, and other African-American establishments, with white perpetrators typically unpunished. It was where Klansmen bombed the Sixteenth Avenue Baptist Church, killing four little girls, with three of assailants not facing justice for decades (the fourth attacker died before he could be brought to trial). Alabama, where former Governor George Wallace declared, "segregation today, segregation tomorrow, segregation forever," grew a special kind of hate. I can only begin to imagine the climate that existed for my father while growing up in that state under Jim Crow, and the motivation that fueled his life-altering move to Flint.

It's also no wonder that my father instilled in us a willingness to stand up to racial discrimination and engage in situations and conversations where some people might be uncomfortable because they involved race.

Knowing what my father went through to get away from Alabama—and what his father went through before dying in Alabama—impacted me. I realized that because of the *Brown v. Board of Education* decision, and the fact that I was born and raised in Flint, Michigan, in the North, I had it a quintillion times better than my granddad and my father did. I had more opportunities than they did, so it was always up to me to take advantage of that. That's how I honor their legacy. That's how I have stood proudly on their shoulders. They paid the price to give me the opportunities that I've had.

Think about the challenge my father would have gone through too in marrying a Puerto Rican. There were challenges in the black community, the Hispanic community, and the white community. But they had a love that was so strong that it overcame so many societal circumstances.

Eli and Julia were married in the living room of my grandmother's house. My father was twenty-one, my mother sixteen—so young that it required my grandmother to accompany them to the courthouse to sign the marriage license. It was a marriage built to last.

I'm so impressed that Julia excelled at two careers. Raising three boys as a stay-at-home mom was a career in itself. Then she became such a factor in teaching special needs kids at my old high school, Flint Southwestern, that she was recognized as the best in the state of Michigan. And she was so modest that she didn't even tell us about her award. I didn't know about the honor until I noticed the award hanging on the wall in the basement during a visit home. At that time, the award was ten years old. She hadn't bothered to put it up earlier.

My mom was always nursing me back to health after so many mishaps during my formative years. That nurturing aspect was something I looked for in a wife and was surely reflected with Marianna, a wonderful mother to our boys. My mom was also extremely supportive, always encouraging me and instilling the idea that education was the key to making my dreams come true. The fact that I was born during the year of the *Brown v. Board of Education* decision not only made

Thurgood Marshall my first hero in life, but it also provided a means for my mother to emphasize that despite being hearing-impaired, despite being African-American, despite being half-Hispanic, despite being relatively poor, through education you can accomplish anything.

Eli was just as inspiring. He was a tremendous example of solid work ethic and entrepreneurial vigor. He worked as a real estate agent for thirty years and owned a taxicab that he would occasionally drive himself. And those were his side gigs. He was one of the first African-Americans to work as a millwright (a highly skilled craftsman) at Fisher Body before becoming a foreman. His thirty-eight years in the auto plants was one reason why I was so sensitive to the long-term effects of the toxic environmental hazards of Spinney Field, the Bengals' headquarters that was situated in an industrial zone in Cincinnati.

My father also turned out to be quite an accomplished golfer as he matured. He was extremely competitive, which is clearly one of the traits that I inherited. But he also taught me something about making adjustments when it came to his game.

In his baseball years he batted right-handed. He was such a strong batter that when he decided to pick up golf, it affected his game. He completely changed his stroke and became a lefty. He played golf from the left side, and it straightened out his hook and everything. That kind of adjustment shows that we sometimes must metamorphose to excel. I saw how he approached his athletic career. He switched sports and did what was necessary to be competitive. I liken that to the different style of linebacker I was during various stages of my career. I adapted my game based on circumstances and the condition of my body. By the end, I wasn't the same type of linebacker that I was when I entered the NFL, when I would hurdle blockers or soar through the air in pursuit of a tackle.

FAMILY

New chapters in our family's history are being written by my sons as we speak, including the impressive athletic exploits of my oldest, Julien. He's competed as a mixed martial arts fighter for more than a decade and is an accomplished trainer and coach of Ultimate Fighting Championship (UFC) fighters. All this from a kid who played point guard in high school. Talk about versatility.

His transition from track and field can be traced to his time at Michigan State, when his roommate was a kid on the wrestling team named Rashad Evans, who was inducted into the UFC Hall of Fame in 2019.

One thing about Julien that is different from me is that he has great sportsmanship. An example: When he won his state title in high school, they got three jumps to determine who would advance to the final for three more jumps. After his last preliminary jump, Julien was in first place. Before the last guy jumped, Julien gave him some advice. The advice was good enough that the guy out-jumped Julien. I was like, "Wow, I would never do that! I would never help the competition!" It pushed Julien to second place. In the final, they both fouled on their first jumps. Julien out-jumped him on the second jump, then they both fouled on their last jumps. Julien won the event, and I was even more proud because he did it in a way that I would not have. He did it with great sportsmanship.

Jarren took his own path to championship glory. He went to the University of Central Florida (UCF) after the football coach, George O'Leary, saw him with me and sized him up, so to speak. At the time, Jarren was a year out of high school and told O'Leary that he wanted to get into college. O'Leary said, "If you try out for the football team and promise not to quit, I'll work to get you admitted into UCF." Jarren made a handshake commitment. I was in Athens for the 2004 Summer

Olympics when I got the call from Jarren, saying that he'd quit the football team. My immediate instinct was to pull him out of school—not because I was pressuring him to play football, but because he went back on his word. UCF kept his admission intact. He never told me, though, that he'd walked on to the wrestling team. I didn't find out until two years after the fact that he'd won two championships. I didn't know about any of his wrestling matches, which was one of the things that was lost to me because I was divorced.

Then there's Kellen, the youngest, who was married in 2019 and has done well launching a career as a wealth manager. Like his brothers, he lives in Orlando. Unlike his brothers, his name doesn't begin with the letter "J"—just one of the distinctions about his birth. He was the only one of the three delivered by natural childbirth. The first two were born in Cincinnati, while Kellen arrived in New York. Marianna's doctor, a black female, refused to give her an epidural. At the end of it, even though I had a "J" name picked out, I was so impressed with my wife that I told her to name him whatever she wanted. She had met Kellen Winslow, the Hall of Fame tight end who later worked with me at Disney, and loved the name.

I contributed Kellen's middle name, Hindry, in an unusual way. My first business trip after his birth took me back to Los Angeles, where I was working on the NFL's YET project. Coming out of LAX airport, I was at a stoplight at Hindry Street when it hit me. Julien and Jarren have religious middle names (Isaiah and Saul, respectively), but Kellen's comes from a street.

Like all families, we've had our share of adversities.

Marianna and I were divorced in 1999 after eighteen years of marriage. The maniacal focus that I had with the business at Disney was a factor, but the biggest concern in going through that type of situation involves the effect it has on the children.

FAMILY

We were divorced right before Julien's senior year in high school. I thought if there was going to be a disconnect with one of my sons, it would be with Kellen, the youngest. I was confident that Julien was old enough and mature enough to understand.

Julien, though, gave me quite a scare not long after I moved out. He took my boat out on Lake Butler, right outside Islesworth. He was waterskiing, with one of his friends driving the boat, and the rope became wrapped around his leg. He got pulled underwater and almost drowned. I had just come back to the empty house to pick up some things from the office. He came through the door with his friend, and I could tell by the expression on their faces that something tragic had happened. I saw Julien's leg. He had a rope burn that went deep into the flesh. He was exhausted and wanted to go to sleep. I knew from my experiences that we had to get him to the hospital as soon as possible to flush out that wound. We rushed to an Urgent Care facility that was closer. If I had not come home, he probably would have gone to lie down, and his leg might have gotten infected, which could have killed him. It was one of those things that reiterated that there were consequences for not being in my own home anymore. The injury impacted his chances of getting a basketball scholarship; he'd been an all-county point guard as a junior. He made a nice comeback in track, though, winning the state championship in his last term.

It was Jarren, though, who had the biggest problem with the divorce. I'm a middle child too. We middle children are a piece of work. The disconnect that I had with him illustrates one of the reasons people often say, after the fact, that if they had to do it all over again, they might not make the same decisions.

Years later, I was there for him in a situation I could have never imagined. It was discovered that Jarren had an irregular heartbeat. To rectify it, they had to stop his heart and then restart it. I was living in Punta Gorda when the situation unfolded but obviously went back to Orlando to be there with him. Having gone through the aorta dissection, I could relate. I'd been on the other side. I could give him fatherly advice before he had to go through one of the scariest things he'd ever have to endure. Stopping your heart—that's got to be scary, okay? It's one of those times when we were really aligned. Thankfully, it worked out well.

It has also been rewarding to witness the relationship that "Uncle Jarren" has developed with Julien's children, Jai and Cassius. *Immense*: That would be the word to describe the love he has for his niece and nephew. I can relate. Gregory's daughter, Mariah—the fashionista of the family—declared years ago and constantly reminds me to this day that she is my "favorite" niece. I'll take that.

Such is the spice of family relationships, which, through thick and thin, are there for life. I'm proud of my family and our history. The good, the bad, the blossoms of the family tree, and even the thorns have all carried me. When I was a child, I knew our family tree was so different than those of my friends. I had no other neighbors, friends, or schoolmates who were half African-American and half Puerto Rican. That's cool too. We come in a lot of different shades.

BOOM BOX: PROTEST OR NOT?

Of course I would have taken a knee during the national anthem if there were such a protest movement in the NFL during my playing days.

Even while serving on the Cincinnati City Council.

In fact, I would have been more compelled to protest as a councilman, given that it was part of my responsibility while serving in public office to provide a voice for people who were silenced, marginalized, or disenfranchised in other ways.

That's why Colin Kaepernick was a kindred spirit. The former San Francisco 49ers quarterback—wrongly blackballed by the NFL, it should be noted—had the right idea in launching his national anthem protest to raise awareness about the problems of the killings of unarmed African-Americans by police and other social injustices.

I can relate.

My worst interaction with police occurred in Orlando during my years as a Disney executive.

One morning after daybreak, I was rushing to see my new girlfriend, who had called in desperation because her ex-husband was threatening her. Along the way, I had an encounter with another driver over the simple matter of the right-of-way at an intersection. As I drove past this driver, I flipped him the finger. He called the police, claiming that I had a gun. Within five minutes, there was a helicopter above me, a fleet of police cars flashing behind me, and a SWAT team tank.

After I stopped, the police approached the car with their guns out. They opened my door, pulled me out, and threw me on the ground. With my face on the asphalt, they put my arms behind me and handcuffed me so tightly that my wrists bled afterward. Then they checked my car, top to bottom. Now if I'd had a gun, I would've gotten my ass beat as the officers—all white—were prepared to teach me a lesson for pulling a gun on a white person. There was no weapon.

Ultimately, after about half an hour, they said, "We're sorry." I was so upset.

I called my peers on the security force at Disney, which has its own police force. We had liaisons whose job it was to collaborate with authorities, including the Orlando Police Department, if we filed a complaint. I didn't follow through with it because I didn't want to create a public distraction for the Happiest Place on Earth. I just dropped it.

But it was a reminder to a black man in America. You could be a vice president at Walt Disney World and an NFL Man of the Year...and still have a gun put to your temple. It's barely a step up from the dogs. Instead of an alpha dog, it's a sergeant. You're eyeballing the number-one guy, and he's ultimately the one who will say, "Arrest him" or "Let him go." But you can't have a normal reaction. You can't act like an upset black dude. You've got be docile.

I never had a chance to explain that I merely flipped the guy the bird.

That's why I can empathize with the protest movement that Kaepernick ignited.

Some might argue that the NFL is an entertainment entity and that its stage is not the place to address all of society's ills. Hogwash. Because of the things that NFL players are asked to do to impact society, and because of causes that the league itself promotes, it is the perfect place to raise awareness with a protest.

FAMILY

My family has also bonded in dealing with the losses of loved ones. When my younger brother Kenny died in 2016 of emphysema, it was by far the toughest phone call—the toughest *moment*—I've ever had. My father had to tell me because my mom was too distraught to even talk.

Kenny was the most accomplished academically among the three of us. After getting his undergraduate degree at Bowling Green, he went on to earn his Ph.D. from the LBJ School of Public Affairs at the University of Texas in Austin. He became a professor at Michigan State and survived long enough to become tenured, fighting racism along the way. He was also a doting father to Katie. Kenny became the classic Mr. Mom while his wife studied in Russia for months at a time. He was also a photographer who inundated us with pictures. One of the reasons that Julien wound up at Michigan State was to build on his relationship with my brother. I visited Kenny several times in East Lansing.

And Kenny was often back in Flint, less than an hour's drive from East Lansing. He wouldn't dare let just any barber cut his hair. It had to be my favorite uncle, Otis, or his son, Otis Jr.—the best barbers on the South Side.

When Kenny passed, my father called me because he had called Greg and Greg wasn't picking up the phone. He called him twice, trying to proceed in the natural family order. He was about to break when he called me. He had to rush to tell me, because my mom had been screaming the whole time, and he was trying to be strong for her. I had to call Greg. It was so shocking that Kenny was dead. It was early in the morning when I finally reached Greg, who lives in Atlanta. He picked up the phone in a good mood. "Hey, what's up, man?" I was crying, but told him what our dad had told me and that I needed him to follow up. He called me back a few minutes later and confirmed everything.

I think about my brother a lot. There are certain things constantly on your heart, and this is one.

A little more than two years after we lost Kenny, we lost my father. I think his years working in the factories was a factor. He worked a variety of jobs that exposed him to a lot of noise, so he had hearing problems. And as we know now, the early factories were contained a lot of asbestos. My father would eventually have two bouts of cancer in his lymph nodes, which ultimately disfigured him at the end. He lost full use of his arm. The cancer came back. His decision at the end was to...you know, "go home." He wasn't going to fight.

He kept teaching me right until the end. He taught me something about amputation because he was prepared to cut off his arm if it might have stopped the cancer. But it was too late. At that stage, he and my mother made a decision in the hospital. I was in Flint, visiting him. He told me that he was "going home" and why. He's the one who told me. That's a father teaching his son. I watch all those National Geographic videos, showing the parents in the animal kingdom raising their young. They teach them how to live and how to survive. But one of the miracles of being human is that we can teach one another how to die. It's the toughest lesson of a lifetime for us all to learn. But rather than grieve about the fact that he's gone, there are so many things I am thankful for when I think about my father now.

His impact on me also fortifies my drive for the legacy that I will leave for my sons and future generations on this family tree. That too has underscored another type of challenge.

CHAPTER 13
COPING

IN MY MIND, MARIJUANA IS A COPING KIND OF DRUG. IT SLOWS things down. It gives you an opportunity to appreciate things that are happening in the moment. It increases your appetite. It increases your ability to sleep. It's a social drug, to the degree that it can increase sexual attraction between consenting adults. And it can do wonders for healing.

During my entire fourteen-year pro football career with the Cincinnati Bengals, I smoked after every single game. At the time, I wasn't thinking of it as medical marijuana, which is at the heart of the case for allowing current NFL players to use it in a fashion that is legal in more than thirty states as a prescription for pain. In my case, it also helped me deal with the stress and anxieties associated with such a high-pressure, high-risk occupation.

In retrospect, I look at the results. How much more has my brain healed than if I hadn't used marijuana? There is no scientific study that I can cite here—such a study hasn't been done for NFL players, from my era or since—but I can speak from my experience and associations with other players. I know a small contingent of players who smoked while playing in the NFL prior to the institution of really strenuous drug testing. Of those roughly two hundred athletes, virtually none of us have Parkinson's or Lou Gehrig's disease. That tells me something.

I do believe, however, that I have chronic traumatic encephalopathy (CTE), which research links to repeated blows to the head—the most severe trauma coming from concussions, the less apparent but perhaps just as dangerous threat coming from sub-concussive hits—that are inherent in football and other sports. Experts conclude that CTE can only be definitively diagnosed posthumously, although researchers are working to develop a test that would confirm the condition in the living. Regardless, I feel the symptoms. Many other former players contend the same. I also believe that CTE is not a death sentence. It's a matter of how you deal with it interpersonally and internally. I wonder whether my CTE symptoms would be worse if I had never smoked marijuana.

I had my first joint as a teenager growing up in Flint, Michigan. It wasn't about pain management then. It was strictly social. Along with some of my buddies, we visited the homes of returning soldiers from Vietnam. Those vets were my high school heroes—the football players from the neighborhood who taught us how to play on the field across the street from my house. If they came back, having survived Vietnam, they were smoking marijuana. And if you went to their house or their room to hear their story, commiserate, and welcome them back, then you couldn't be the person that was not going to puff and pass. That's where it all started. It was always a sort of badge of fellowship. Smoking pot wasn't as criminal at that time as it later became. This was in the late '60s. Back then, when I arrived on campus at Dartmouth, the brother that I stayed with—we all stayed with hosts—was getting high. I had one of the best nights of my life the first time I visited Dartmouth College. I smoked some of the best stuff I had ever had. Throughout my whole undergraduate years, I smoked, whether it was on campus or off campus, whether I found it in Mexico City or in San Diego.

But over fifty years, I have certainly evolved from merely rolling a joint. Now, in managing pain linked to the surgeries and assorted health issues I have encountered—including my determined battle to save my right leg from amputation—I swear by transdermal patches bolstered with cannabidiol (CBD) and tetrahydrocannabinol (THC) in addition to having a fat doobie.

Soon after my aortic dissection in 2014, which resulted in unexpected progress with my hip, the last remaining pain was even more irritating, more frustrating. In trying to combat that, I hurt myself—overdoing it with rehab again—and wound up back on crutches. A friend of mine who ran a marijuana dispensary, another Dartmouth classmate, gave me a goodie box with a variety of medical cannabis products to try, to see if anything would work. That was the first time I used the patches. If you're smoking marijuana while using the patches, you don't notice the patches. What I did notice, though, was when I had the patches on, I had less pain. When I didn't have the patches on, the pain came back. I went back to him for more patches. About three months later, he left the company for another job, but he put me in touch with the owner, Chad Connors. That led to me becoming an endorser of their product. In exchange for endorsing their patches, I received stock in the San Diego-based company, Pure Ratios. That makes me an owner of a company I believe in. That was before the State of Florida passed all its medical marijuana laws. After legalization measures passed in Florida, I got my medical marijuana card from Dr. Barry Gordon, who has a place, Compassionate Cannabis, in Venice. The Florida medical marijuana dispensaries are not as expansive as those I've seen in California or that I've heard exist in Colorado, but marijuana's legal here and I'm not a criminal anymore.

As much as it helps with the aches, it may be even more essential in healing brain injuries, as some research suggests, and in treating CTE.

How do I know that I have CTE?

There's no question I fit the profile. I was diagnosed three times with concussions while playing in the NFL. Actually, my first concussion came during adolescence, when I fell out of a tree, so I've had at least four. What I'm not counting are a whole bunch of cases where I was dazed after a collision on the football field. And I'm not accounting for an array of stingers either. Also, we played with helmets far inferior to what players wear today. We wore those suspension helmets with very little padding. The rules were different back then too, when it was common for guys to use their heads in making a tackle. When you snapped on that chinstrap, you were all about business.

In fourteen years in the NFL as a full-contact linebacker, that's a lot of hard-hitting business.

What is the differentiation between having symptoms and having CTE? In my view, it's medical certainty. If you think you have it, based on symptoms, you probably have it. CTE is confirmed by the levels of tau protein in the brain, but there are currently no tests to measure this in living patients. So, the key to understanding whether you have it begins with recognizing the symptoms.

One of the symptoms is heightened emotionality. Almost every day, sitting outside where I smoke my morning doobie,

I'll break into tears because of the slightest trigger. I'll read a feel-good story, a good-little-dog story, or some inspirational story where someone is making a difference, and I'll become emotional. Most of it is empathy; I feel the pain of every other person's experience. Or it could be reading about Megan Rapinoe and the fact that she is willing to be an ally. It could be any of those things that really hit me. The flip side of it is, I don't read about Donald Trump anymore because it makes me angry. It inflames something inside my heart.

That's another symptom I must be aware of. I get hot flashes of anger. That's why I had to leave Punta Gorda. During the election cycle in 2016, I had rages every night. I don't have the ability to back down from a good argument. You've got to walk away or not get into it in the first place. I'm not the type to walk away, so I might as well not get into it in the first place. The mood swings, the red-hot flashes are the uncontrollable aspects. You can lose a little bit of your self-control.

Sure, I had a fiery temper when I was younger, like when I got into fights on a daily basis during my rookie Bengals training camp. But that was cause and effect. There was no premeditated "I'm in a bad mood today, and the first person who crosses this line gets it." It was circumstantial, situational. I've lost it on the football field. I've gotten unsportsmanlike-conduct penalties, but it happens and then it's over. But this is different, it's beyond my control. Once you get in that anger mode, you've got to resolve what is angering you, and then you're going to continue to argue. And I was getting too close to blows when it came to the subject of politics and Trump. I've never been in a real street fight, and I sure don't want to get into one now. I wouldn't trust myself in a real street fight.

I don't want to hate anyone. But you've got to hate some-one who is anti-healthcare. It is such a point of privilege for any rich billionaire to think that there are other Americans—fellow citizens who elected him to office—who don't deserve healthcare. How can a leader of this country have that kind of mentality for something so critical to the nexus of a society? We're the only country that bankrupts its citizens because of medical expenses.

Believe me, I know a few things about healthcare, medi-cal expenses, and the red tape that comes with it. The men-tal anguish I've endured over several years while dealing with health issues has undoubtedly contributed to my CTE symptoms.

Since my bilateral knee replacement in 2005, the chal-lenges have included: paying in the high six-figures in out-of-pocket expenses; being dropped for insurance coverage; a legal battle against the Bengals over worker's compensation; denial of Social Security benefits; limited insurance coverage with a rider that wouldn't cover the preexisting condition of my ravaged right knee; minimal support from the NFL and NFLPA, with their labor deal excluding retirees like myself who played before 1993 from the lifetime medical benefits afforded current players and more recent retirees; exhaustive battles with hospitals over billing disputes and practices. All that, and a few more health scares to boot. The bone infection that nearly cost me my leg returned in 2018 after being dor-mant for eleven years. And 2019 began with more surgeries as my prosthetic right knee was removed and replaced by a concrete spacer. I have surely been tested many times over. Again. And still.

Despite the CTE symptoms and adversity, I try to maintain a positive disposition. Otherwise, once you get into the spiral of depression, it's hard to excavate yourself. When an infection returns that you thought was long gone, that's depression waiting to happen. I was at a point where I felt I had achieved the happy ending that was my goal despite all the sacrifices. The pain was getting better. Then the worst thing that could happen, happened.

The infection erupted again in November 2018. After eleven years, the osteomyelitis came back even stronger, rejecting the antibiotics that had worked previously. This became evident when the wound would not close. The wound stayed open for an entire month. After they readmitted me in January, they had to cut away some more of the flesh to try to get past the necrotic tissue. I had to come to grips with the possibility that despite surviving the previous threats of amputation, the leg would not be saved this time.

I received the grim news from Dr. Alexis Sockwell, who recommended amputation after efforts to treat the infection hit a standstill. My mom had come down to Sarasota from Flint and was with me in the doctor's office as I talked to Sockwell. I didn't want to act shocked or scared as he talked about taking off the leg, so I went down that rabbit hole with him: *What does this mean? When are you talking about doing it? Are there any other options?* My mom didn't say anything the whole time, but it was the closest I came to accepting that I would lose the leg. Yet just as I was going through that litany of questions, my mind kind of accepting the inevitability but still resistant to it, Dr. Sean Dingle came into the room and said, "I've got another choice."

Man, that was like hearing the cavalry coming. Dingle talked about conservatively going back into the leg and instead of cutting it off, doing another abrasion of all the necrotic tissue, washing the cavity out, and replanting another concrete spacer—which keeps my leg straight between the tibia and the femur—that contained a different antibiotic. It was the last shot to save the leg. And it was a miracle. Bactrim, the latest and greatest antibiotic, turned out to be the solution that could kill or repress the growth of the infection.

Months after that surgery, it seemed so fitting that when I ran into Sockwell by chance in downtown Sarasota, he was wearing a Superman T-shirt. He did a Superman job in finally closing that wound. The wound stayed healed and is healthy now.

The original projection was to keep the spacer in place for slightly less than a year before replacing it with another prosthetic. My range of motion in the right leg is about 60 degrees, which is about three inches, allowing me heel to toe movement. I can walk. The challenge during the surgery, however, was that they could barely remove the last prosthetic. They had to cut higher on the femur to try to bend the leg because of all the bone spurs. The other option was to fuse the bone so I wouldn't be able to bend the leg—although I could put all my weight on it and walk on it. I'd have to walk another way, swinging the leg around like you see the runners with a prosthetic do in a distance race. That would have been something else I'd have to learn.

Yet nine months after the spacer was inserted came the wonderful news of an unexpected result: no surgery. Bone spurs grew to cover the spacer. The knee had fused itself. There was no need to replace the concrete spacer with a titanium spacer. There was no need to put my immune system through another surgery. This spacer will be in there forever. But I guarantee I'll get stopped by the TSA people at the airport every time.

Of course, one thing led to another. The latest round included back pain that was so severe I couldn't walk to the local restaurants that I like to frequent. A guy who at one point couldn't imagine cooking for himself suddenly had to cook every day. I had to learn to adjust. At first, they couldn't figure out where the back pain was coming from. They thought it was kidney stones, then concluded that I had a sodium imbalance. Taking the Bactrim negatively affected my kidneys. I always drink a lot of water, but the more water you drink, the more you're diluting the antibiotics. Part of the fix was drinking less water. It was a whole change in consumption. It worked. My first blood test and check of my vitals showed they were within the normal range. And my back began hurting less and less.

Unfortunately, that wasn't the only pain. Settling the medical bills with the hospitals for surgeries on an uninsured knee represented another type of drama that lasted for months. The total for that out-of-pocket expense was staggering. And the itemization of those costs was overwhelming, which is why I hired someone to negotiate the case on my behalf. Even worse, I felt like I was being treated as though I was just a number and not a human being. The hospital initially wouldn't recognize my representative and refused to deal with her. I called them, gave them information, and signed a legal paper designating her to proceed on my behalf. They still refused to return her repeated calls. The frustration and sense that I was being screwed over—on top of all those years with the surgical procedures, medical costs, and discomfort—became overwhelming. And once you're feeling overwhelmed, it's hard to simultaneously adopt a positive demeanor about yourself and everything around you. When I was an executive at Walt Disney World, I loved negotiating in the spirit of finding a win-win scenario for both sides. But part of the issue in this case is that I've been successful enough that I can't get a subsidy from Obamacare, and I can't really get a subsidy from a hospital based upon my net worth.

The system that dictates healthcare costs and the practices of the insurance industry are so out of control. At no point in the hospital do you even get an option to say what you want or don't want. There are things in the hospital you are charged for that provide very little value toward what you're there for, but the costs are still added to the bill because insurance companies are going to pay for it. Then insurance companies raise their premiums and deny more policies for more conditions while hedging their bets as an industry.

Then there's this whole Trump dismantling of Obamacare. It gives existing insurance companies the green light to play hardball. That's where we are. There's no conscience now in the insurance industry. And it's been moving in this direction for some time.

You're kidding? That was my reaction after my insurance was canceled in 2009 as I was rehabbing from my third right-knee replacement. The reaction came upon learning that my costs were significantly worse than my worst-case fears. It was the realization that money I had earned with the goal of leaving an inheritance for my three sons would be significantly depleted. Money that I'm paying to a hospital is money that I won't be able to leave to my kids.

After retiring from Disney, I maintained the excellent insurance plan (that had covered my bilateral knee replacement surgery in 2005) for a year and a half with a COBRA policy. If you're disabled and want to be able to continue to buy that insurance, you have to go to Social Security and claim a disability, which is what I did in 2009. I was always going to have a handicapped existence because of my leg. But they denied my disability based upon the determination that, as an executive in corporate America at Disney, I didn't need my legs. I was punished because I was a successful executive in corporate America. I was on the diversity committee, so I know we hired many cast members in wheelchairs. From a Social Security standpoint there was a logic there, but it was totally unfair.

That put me at the mercy of the market. With a preexisting knee condition, the premiums for covering me in 2009 were $5,000 to $6,000. A month. And the quote I got was the Obamacare quote. If I'd bought the Disney insurance, it would have cost about $3,000 a month.

My girlfriend at the time, Sil Lai Abrams, wound up finding me a policy based purely on price. What I didn't know was that it came with a rider that stipulated they would not cover any problem with my leg for ten years. I didn't know. Preexisting condition.

There are a lot of things they have covered. They covered the stroke. They covered the aortic dissection. They covered two operations on my feet, which I had when I was trying to walk without lifts in my legs. Initially, I was in denial that my right leg was three inches shorter than the left. My belief was that if I unlocked my hip, that's where my missing distance would come from. It was only after three or four years that I had shoes made with an altered heel to equalize the length of my legs. Before that, the task of walking with that difference in length between one leg and the other created bone spurs between my baby toe and the next-smallest toe. Ultimately, those spurs broke through the skin, got infected, and I had to get them cut out. The insurance company covered that.

I pursued the worker's compensation case against the Bengals in California in 2009, at the time of my greatest need. Although the case was ultimately resolved with a small settlement, the team fought me vigorously. They simply didn't want to be responsible for costs associated with repairing or otherwise treating a knee that had been damaged while going all-out on the field.

It's all based on their philosophy. There are clubs who are taking care of their players. The former owner of the 49ers, Eddie DeBartolo, is one prime example. But Mike Brown obviously has a different view. It's quirky. I've had many wonderful experiences with Brown (the former Dartmouth quarterback) over the years. I was a pallbearer at the funeral for his legendary father, Paul. He facilitated my opportunity as general manager of the New York/New Jersey Knights of the World League of American Football. And I've received correspondence from him over the years, congratulating me on one achievement after another during my life after the Bengals.

Yet this is where we'll never see eye to eye. I absolutely disagree with his position that he has to treat all players the same when it comes to fighting worker's compensation claims. Not every player did what I did. Not every player played more than two hundred games for his franchise. If you were ever going to justify an exception, I should have ranked as worthy. My point to Brown was this: At the end of the day, what do you want the result to be? Do you want me to go through what I'm going through? For all that you know about the knee injuries that I sustained?

Brown was part of the decision-making in 1986 when I underwent the postseason abrasion surgery on my right knee, which was the forerunner to microfracture surgery. He said they would support me. The only thing: I never got it in writing.

Then again, if players from my era had lifetime health-care coverage, many issues would have been avoided. When I crossed the picket line during the NFL players strike in 1987, maintaining that healthcare was a more important issue than free agency, maybe I had some premonition of what I would face decades later. I certainly feared the potential for some of these financially ruinous cases that have wreaked havoc on pre-'93 retirees.

But I never projected this. Not with the inflation of health-care costs. There's no way I could have imagined that a surgery on my leg would eventually cost as much as four years of NFL income. Had I known that in '87, I would have said, "Guys, I'm going to tell you, you might prefer free agency right now, but if you get cancer or have what I have, you're going to spend more money than you'll earn through free agency because health-care costs are going to get out of control." No one could have convinced me that my medical cost for a knee operation was going to be 2,000 percent higher in ten years.

That's why I've been all in on supporting efforts to increase benefits for the pre-'93 class of retirees, who don't have a seat at the bargaining table when the NFL and the players union negotiate their labor agreements. This class is dependent on external pressure and the goodwill of owners and union leaders to live up to their pledge to support older retirees.

The NFL has established various plans designated to financially assist players dealing with a variety of issues, including those related to neurological conditions generally associated with head trauma. But it is a steep bar to hurdle, given the red tape and denial rates that make it difficult for the retirees and their families to receive relevant support.

Simply put, all retired NFL players—regardless of the era that they played—should be entitled to the lifetime health-care benefits that the current players are eligible to receive. To insure the entire pre-'93 class of retirees, the yearly premiums would probably cost less than Roger Goodell's annual salary as NFL commissioner. Instead, the costs are being passed on to the American taxpayer as older retirees are typically left to wait until they can qualify for Medicare.

I'm on Medicare. The difference is that for a $100,000 medical bill, for instance, the Medicare cost is a third of that. The extra $70,000 the doctors and hospitals charge in non-Medicare cases is because they are getting an insurance company to reimburse them.

The billing process now typically involves two different costs—one being a lesser amount negotiated for insurance. Well, the hospitals are going after the patient for the difference between what the insurance companies will pay and the actual bill. A lot of doctors and hospitals are padding their bills. I hired someone with the expertise to do the negotiations and to let me know the bottom line.

I'm hopeful that my experiences in dealing with my issues—including the trials with the healthcare industry—can benefit others. That's been part of the mission in sharing my story. While it has certainly been therapeutic to reflect, running the gamut from nostalgia to hard-core venting, it is even more imperative to leave something behind from my journey—be it information, perspective, or even entertainment—that represents value. I want to be a conduit for the type of inspiration that I have received along the way and to make a difference.

COPING

If there's one lesson I've learned, it's this: Have resilience. We must never give up in the face of our greatest challenges. That's the essence of living life to the fullest.

BOOM BOX: WHY THE NFL SHOULD "LEGALIZE" MARIJUANA

We are way into overtime with the idea that the NFL should "legalize" marijuana. Never mind that marijuana is still classified by the feds as a Schedule 1 drug. At the start of 2020, thirty-three states allowed cannabis for medicinal purposes, which is precisely why it should be allowed for NFL players.

In lieu of completely removing marijuana from the list of banned substances in the NFL drug policy, it was encouraging to see the league and the NFLPA take a page from the NBA's playbook in their new collective bargaining agreement and adjust the levels to loosen the testing standard for what constitutes a positive result. It's about time. The revised policy included in the 11-year extension of the labor that was struck in March 2020, allows players a non-opioid option for dealing with the pain absorbed in their brutal profession.

The revision also dictates a more supportive approach that revolves around treatment rather than punitive discipline for those who enter the drug program for flunking marijuana tests. And at the levels now pre-scribed, it's doubtful that players using marijuana as a pain-reliever—or, too, as recreational users—would test positive in the numbers that they have for many years.

Kudos, NFL and NFLPA. That's what I would have done... years ago.

A few years ago, I told NFL commissioner Roger Goodell as much and even asked to be invited to any internal think-tank sessions to vouch for the benefits of cannabis as a pain-relief option.

Goodell never followed up with me. But thankfully, the issue didn't go away as marijuana becomes more widely accepted in society. But the league's position for the longest time was that they were "studying the research."

Knowledge should indeed drive decision-making. I thought way before now they should have been able to say definitively why they didn't allow it. To my understanding, they didn't have a reason other than to say it's on the federal list. And it was a control mechanism. Another thumb on the pulse of the player.

With the NFL following in the footsteps of the NBA and Major League Baseball (which expanded its relaxed policy in December 2019) in effectively removing cannabis from their lists of banned substances, I believe the Olympics, Major League Soccer and women's soccer will follow suit. Someone needs to be the leader in making it more acceptable to use marijuana for medical purposes. The NFL has the kind of ratings that can make the point even stronger than the NBA can. If they didn't revise the policy in the new labor deal it would have been a travesty.

When I think about the things we've already learned about cannabis—its benefits in treating Parkinson's disease, liver disease, glaucoma, and for pain management—I wonder, "Why is it illegal?" And it's so much less expensive than all those outrageous medical bills from for-profit companies that raise their prices every single year. That's why we're in this ridiculous upward spiral of healthcare costs, and one of the solutions to the problem is another industry that produces cannabis.

The NFL chose to be ignorant for so long. When I talked to Mike Brown about it several years ago, I remember him telling me, "Oh, that's interesting. That's new information, but I've never been told that."

Like other former players–including Chris Long, a fellow former NFL Man of the Year who has spoken out on the issue–I can vouch for the benefits. Marijuana helped me endure fourteen years in the NFL. Smoking it was the first thing I did when I got home from every single game in which I played. If it was a home game, I would never smoke in the car. But once I got home, behind closed doors, it was the first thing I did. It helped me mentally rewind the ebbs and flows of the game, along with taking my mind off the consequences of injury. You hear about people having these near-death experiences, where they feel like they are out of their body and looking at themselves. That is sort of the benefit I got. I was able to separate myself from my pain and discomfort and look at them dispassionately. It was always a cushion. That's why I rarely took any kind of pain pill after a game.

The NFL started drug testing around 1983, probably as a consequence of the '82 strike. Until then, they didn't test for marijuana. But after it became part of the policy, you could avoid random testing if you passed an annual test that you knew was coming by staying clean for thirty days. I hated those thirty days. But it worked. I never flunked a drug test. All these years later, though, they've come around to acknowledge a better way to deal with marijuana in the NFL drug policy: Just say yes.

EPILOGUE

IN THE MIDDLE OF THE NIGHT, JUST BEFORE THANKSGIVING in 2019, Reggie Williams lay on the floor of his penthouse apartment with virtually no option except to wait. He was in agony again, with a fractured right hip. What happened? While navigating through the dark, Reggie lost his balance as he tripped over one of his customized shoes strewn on the floor. He made a split-second decision to absorb the crash on his side rather than try breaking the fall with his arms.

"As soon as it hit," he recalled a few weeks later, "I knew it was broken."

He also knew exactly what he needed to do next. He crawled from his bedroom to the kitchen, collected ice, then scooted back to treat the injury and wait out the night. After one o'clock in the morning, he concluded it was fruitless to summon help. The security system at his condominium that allows residents to electronically buzz in guests through the main entrance was inoperable with the building undergoing renovation. At daybreak, after the concierge came on duty, Karen Sweat, a longtime pal from his Dartmouth days, came to help Reggie gather pertinent materials needed for another trip to the hospital. We all need friends like that.

EPILOGUE

Yet for several hours, Reggie let it sink in during a long night. Just when it appeared he had entered a certain comfort zone following another health scare—the year had begun with a fourth right-knee replacement and insertion of a concrete spacer after a bone infection reemerged—another issue was born. Life is fragile like that, especially for Reggie, whose body has known trauma all too well as a companion.

What Reggie refused to do while processing his new twist in the middle of the night was wallow in self-pity. As he put it, "It was not a woe-is-me moment."

That's the essence of the man I've come to know in the year that we've collaborated on his memoir. Sure, throughout his life, he's certainly had moments of despair. After all, even though he jokes that his right leg is bionic—a long titanium rod was inserted during the hip surgery, to complement the concrete in his prosthetic knee—he's human. But temporary bouts with gloom have been no match for the can-do spirit that he has repeatedly tapped to win at life.

"If someone had to turn this ultra-negative into an ultra-positive, that's my history," Reggie declared. "That's this book. It's like I've got one more test to prove the validity of what I'm writing about."

Resilience. Reggie didn't need to prove it again. If there was such a thing as the National Bounce Back Club, he'd be the chairman. But no need to squash the thought. He's on a roll.

Listen to him reflect on the hip surgery when a member of the surgical team wore a customized scrub hat bearing the logo of the Pittsburgh Steelers. As he was being prepped to be sedated, he thought, "You've got to be kidding me? A *Steelers fan* is going to cut on me?"

Then, of course, "I was knocked out within five minutes," he added.

Within two months of that operation, Reggie was driving, and walking without crutches. He was pleased by a particular negative-to-positive result: after battling sciatica for eleven years—the "maddening pain" stemming from the sciatic nerve shot through his hip, lower back and leg—the condition vanished after the hip surgery. That added fuel to his rehab, when he was hell-bent to hit specific targets. Done and done. It helped to work with the type of physical therapist that he didn't always have in other situations due to insurance issues, but he swore that the foundation of his rehab always flows from the training regimen he learned from former Cincinnati Bengals conditioning coach Kim Wood upon entering the NFL in 1976.

"I've been a little bit in seclusion for the last decade, trying to walk again," Reggie says. "I've had to be my own personal trainer, my own drill sergeant. I tell myself, 'One more rep.' In solitude, I don't hear somebody else at the end of a workout, saying, 'Good job.'"

It's striking to Reggie that the hip injury occurred less than three weeks after he stood at the 50-yard line at Yankee Stadium as the greatest football player in Dartmouth College history, feted by school president Philip Hanlon during ceremonies at halftime of a clash against Ivy League rival Princeton as they commemorated 150 years of college football.

The trip to New York came shortly after he was cleared to travel, or as he figures, to make the "once-in-one-hundred-fifty-year occasion." He had a blast of a visit, particularly with the time spent with Thomas Price, the Dartmouth alum who was once one of his team doctors during his GM days in the World League of American Football.

During the course of his life, Reggie has earned no shortage of honors. But now, as he crosses his mid-sixties, I've wondered whether the accolades are more special to him at this stage of life. For all the physical challenges he's endured, including the litany of episodes to save his right leg from amputation, maybe the appreciation is a type of psychological counterbalance.

"When people say, 'Is it worth it?'" Reggie says, alluding to the health issues, "the appreciation reminds you of what you've accomplished and why it was worth it. It really resonates more, though, now that my father has passed away. The things that he drove me to accomplish, I have accomplished in my life."

We should all take the opportunity to reflect on our lives and ponder decisions along the way as Reggie has, absorbing the lessons and fully grasping the pivotal moments of our journey. Reggie wonders what might have happened had he given up football coming out of high school and attended the University of Michigan to pursue a medical career. Or how much more of an impact would he have had on the city of Cincinnati had he remained in the community?

One thing for certain: Reggie is not a man carrying many regrets.

"There's a yin-yang to decision-making," he says. "There's a cost to every decision, and sometimes that cost is bigger than the return on that decision. But you live and learn from those decisions. In the aggregate, every single decision I've made I've followed a logical sequence of decision-making. At the end of the day, I can't regret anything, although I would regret anything that would lead me to amputation of my leg.

"I've even been challenged on that: 'Well, what if we took three hundred thousand dollars from you? Would you feel the same way? We'll put a price on what you believe.' That's the situation I've been in. Even though I wasn't trying to make that decision, I want my leg even more. Now there's a price on it, and I've been forced to pay it. Thank God, I've made enough right decisions in terms of my retirement nest egg that I'll be able to absorb this and still provide the inheritance that I desire for my three sons. It's just not going to be as much money for them to divide."

Yes, Reggie would do his football career all over again. Never mind that he believes he is dealing with symptoms of chronic traumatic encephalopathy and he calls his right leg "a mosaic of scars," from so many surgeries.

"There's this kind of common knowledge that an NFL player on average lives to fifty-seven years old," he says. A study led by a group of researchers at Harvard's T. H. Chan School of Public Health, published in 2019 by *JAMA Network Open*, concluded that 3,419 former NFL players over a thirty-five-year period beginning in 1979, had an average age at death of 59.6 years.

"So as I played, my demeanor was predicated on a limited time that I'm going to be on this Earth. That mentality would have interfered with my objectivity in looking at concussions... and now I'm experiencing the consequences. But I'd still do it over again, in large part because I have exceeded the expected lifetime. In that respect, all the aches and pains are the learnings of the challenge of living. It's a different kind of game, a different opponent, a different scoring system. And every day you can be defeated, or you can be a champion. Every day, I'm trying to triumph over all this adversity. Every day, every issue, one at a time."

It has been clear in reflecting with Reggie just how adamant he is to have his say on his legacy. He's left some footprints that he doesn't want to fade over time. There's no shame in that. In some ways, however, he's been almost excessive about it. Take the 1977 game against the Steelers. Reggie recalled securing a fumble that led to an exchange that drew a flag on "Mean" Joe Greene for hurling the football at him. When I checked the official play-by-play summary from the game, though, another player was credited with the fumble recovery.

Decades later, Reggie wanted to know what it would take for an official statistical correction. Talk about passion.

He still grumbles about the end of Super Bowl XXIII, when defensive coordinator Dick LeBeau left him on the bench as the 49ers marched to a last-minute, game-winning touchdown. He loves LeBeau but held that coaching decision against him for some time.

I mentioned it to LeBeau in early 2020, during a break in our marathon meeting when we were members of a blue-ribbon panel that selected the centennial class for the Pro Football Hall of Fame. LeBeau was stunned to hear it. Out of respect, Reggie had never told LeBeau about his angst from that Super Bowl.

"I am so sorry," LeBeau said. "I must've had brain lock. I don't even remember that he wasn't on the field at the end. It was an oversight. He should have been in there."

Small consolation now, but at least LeBeau owned up to it.

"Tell Reggie," LeBeau added, "that I hope he hasn't forgotten all of those special defenses that I designed for him."

LeBeau went on to contend that If Reggie played in today's NFL, with his combination of speed and power as a rush linebacker, he would dominate.

There has been so much to unpack from Reggie's eventful life. It's no wonder that during the final stages of the process, he kept dropping names that he wanted to acknowledge. You can't say the man doesn't care about people.

Like Jimmie Lee Solomon. A former Alpha Phi Alpha fraternity brother at Dartmouth, Solomon went on to become the highest-ranking African-American executive in Major League Baseball. Years ago, Reggie and Solomon were photographed by *Black Enterprise* magazine for a feature on "The 15 Most Important Blacks in Sports."

Solomon was also the engine who drove the Civil Rights Game in Cincinnati that helped generate attention for the Underground Railroad Freedom Center.

"That game has sort of gone away as Jimmie went away from MLB," Reggie said. "It was a great gesture. Unless I'm missing something, that's something the NFL doesn't do but should do, to honor the legacy of African-Americans in the sport."

Reggie is such a treasure trove of knowledge, wisdom, and insight. Try as he might, he will never be completely finished crossing off his checklist of ideas, opinions, and people to praise. Something else always pops into mind, which is part of the spice of his life about now.

"This has been therapeutic," he said, "but it's also like, 'What have I forgotten?'"

Nonetheless, this is the right time to tell his story.

"I was always waiting for a happy ending," he said. "Then just as I thought I was on the verge of one, that's when another calamity struck. That's where the lessons of life are crystallized."

Lessons that Reggie has shown us can be lived well.

—Jarrett Bell

ACKNOWLEDGMENTS

THIS TSUNAMI OF GRATITUDE ONLY BEGINS TO REFLECT THE waves of love and support that I have received from so many, in various situations over the course of my life. I am truly humbled by what people have done for me in ways that mere words cannot express enough. The least I can do is to try by saying thank you to:

- Monroe, my dad's father. Every pain that I have experienced, I compare the gravity against a man who died early at fifty-two, before I was born, from the accumulated toll of Jim Crow in his lifetime. I have always been in such awe that despite harsh conditions, he raised a loving family.
- Big Mama, for surviving Alabama of the '40s and '50s.
- Elijah and Julia Williams, who raised me and my two brothers in Flint, Michigan, a hometown that I love. They were the best parents, loving us all equally and unconditionally. What a model for me to follow.
- My three sons, Kellen, Jarren, and Julien, the father to my two grandchildren, Jai and Cassius. What tremendous blessings I have received in all of you.

- Marianna, the mother of my children.
- Andrea and Char, wonderful daughters-in-law.
- Greg, my older brother, who has always maintained style points.
- Kenny, my smartest younger brother. May he rest in heaven.
- Mariah, my favorite niece, with Katie being a perfect complement.
- Uncles Otis and Moses, Aunts Sadie and Sandra and many others from the Williams and Casellas families.
- Jarrett Bell. In collaborating to complete this bucket-list item, I talked to him more than any family member for the better part of a year. JB is now my brother for life.
- Russell Wilson. What a touching foreword about the deep friendship I had with his dad, Harry B. HB's oldest brother and my favorite Dartmouth College Board of Trustees member, Benjamin Wilson, and Harry IV and Tammy were helpful too in facilitating communications.
- Post Hill Press, for your belief in this book, with special love for Debby Englander, who heard part of my story and signed me up to hear the rest.
- Georgia Court, owner of Bookstore One in Sarasota. A Cincinnati native, she helped me feel at home, and invited me to participate in the community conversation with Elsie Scott, where Debby just happened to be there listening.
- The Disney family, past and present, including: Michael Eisner, who first saw my potential; Judson Green and Al Weiss, who hired me; Lee Cockerell, the best boss you can imagine; Phil Lengyel, may he rest in peace; thousands of

cast members who continue to make ESPN Wide World of Sports the best youth sports complex in the world; original sportscast members Marilyn Alexander, Bob Glinka, Debbie Shannon (the first hired employee who did everything that I didn't do), and Ruth Robles.

— The late, great Paul, Pete (RIP), and Mike Brown, for drafting me to become a Cincinnati Bengal.

— Great Bengals coaches Forrest Gregg and Sam Wyche (who are missed), along with Kim Wood and Dick LeBeau.

— Teammates from the winningest era of Bengals franchise history, and especially: Ken Riley, Isaac Curtis, Jim LeClair (RIP), Louis Breeden, Anthony Muñoz, Max Montoya, Cris Collinsworth, Boomer Esiason, Joe Kelly, Bobby Kemp (RIP), Ross Browner, Eddie Edwards, Archie Griffin, Ken Anderson, Kevin Walker, Solomon Wilcots, Ickey Woods, and Mike Martin.

— The Dartmouth College football program. Congratulations for winning another Ivy League Championship in 2019. Appreciation too to head coach Buddy Teevens for the Reggie Williams Award, to my head coach, Jake Crouthamel (RIP), President Dartmouth College Phil Hanlon, Athletic Director Harry Sheehy, Asst. A.D. Sam Hopkins, wrestling coach Jerry Berndt, and Mike Slive (RIP). Legends Willie Bogan, Stuart Simms, and Murray Bowden. And much respect to Steve Hatchell and all at the College Football Hall of Fame.

— Alpha Phi Alpha, Theta Zeta Chapter, and special frat brothers Ron and Don Smith (RIP), Grayland Crisp, Lenny Nichols (RIP), Steve White, Frank Turner, Jimmie Lee Solomon, and Ken Mickens.

- The Cincinnati City Council, including aides Susan Silver and Yvonne Thomas.
- Rick "Stick" Taylor, my best friend during the formative years in Flint.
- Zuri Cudjloe and all the fashion talent at Robert Graham.
- Vince and Lucy Payne, and Isaac Eger, whose assistance was invaluable after I broke my hip.
- My village of doctors: Steve O'Brien, Tom Price, Mark Sand, Sean Dingle, Ed Stolarski, Rob Knego, Manny Gordillo, Tom Winters, Robert Heitz Sr., Robert Heitz, Jr., Reggie Tall, Alex DeJesus, Alexis Sockwell, Ken Leone, Barry Brause, Barry Gordon, Frank Jobe, Jason Spector, and Saeed Shahzad. Cheers too to special nurses Jenni Dolphin and Karen Bush.

* * * * *

COLLABORATOR JARRETT BELL WISHES TO THANK THE FOLlowing for assistance and/or support: Rachel Shuster, Debby Englander, Darrell Fry, Carl Gilliard, Teri McFadden, Geoff Hobson, Jemele Hill, George Willis, John Turney, Joe Horrigan, Jack Brennan, Carlton Stowers, Roscoe Nance (RIP), Russell Wilson, Ben Wilson, Lane Gammel, Mark Rodgers, Heather King, Daniel Schuette, Larry Lundy, Julia Williams, Moses Williams, Sadie Williams, Burt Lauten, Angela Tegnelia, Cyrus Mehri, Karen Bryant, Clarence Hill, Michael Silver, Risa Balayem, Tom O'Toole, and Jasmine Bell and her brother, Jalen Bell, the perfect sounding board for sparking the creative process.